Pennsylvania Guide to Real Estate Licensing Examinations

Ronald M. Friedman, J.D., is a member of the bar in both Pennsylvania and New Mexico. He is engaged in the private practice of real estate law, teaches in the Professional Real Estate Development Program at The Pennsylvania State University, and is a licensed broker. He is a coauthor with Benjamin N. Henszey of the book *Real Estate Law*, published by Warren, Gorham & Lamont.

Pennsylvania Guide to Real Estate Licensing Examinations

For Salespersons and Brokers

Ronald M. Friedman
Member of the Pennsylvania Bar

WARREN, GORHAM & LAMONT
Boston and New York

210 South Street
Boston, Massachusetts 02111

ISBN 0-88262-415-6

Library of Congress Catalog Card Number 79-48053

PRINTED IN THE UNITED STATES OF AMERICA

Contents

Preface

The applicant for either the salesperson or broker licensing examination is required to pass a written test comprising two sections. The first section consists of 100 questions dealing with general aspects of real estate, including real estate law, theory and practice, and brokerage. This part of the examination is sometimes referred to as the "uniform" portion because similar tests are administered not only in Pennsylvania but in many other states as well. The questions are standard ones and do not take into account variations among the principles, practices, or laws of the several states. Successful completion of the uniform portion of the examination requires a thorough understanding of basic real estate principles. For a book designed to assist in preparation for the uniform portion of the examination, see French, Martin, and Battle, *Guide to Real Estate Licensing Examinations for Salespersons and Brokers* (Boston and New York: Warren, Gorham & Lamont, 1978).

The second portion of the examination consists of 30 questions dealing only with Pennsylvania statutory law and with rules and regulations issued by the Pennsylvania Real Estate Commission. This portion of the examination is sometimes referred to as the "state," or license law, portion. The laws and regulations of each state vary widely, and in order to successfully complete the Pennsylvania examination, it is necessary to have a good working knowledge of the law and the rules and regulations effective in Pennsylvania.

The brokerage, purchase, sale, and leasing of real estate in the Commonwealth of Pennsylvania are regulated by the Pennsylvania Real Estate Licensing Act of 1980 and the rules and regulations of the Pennsylvania Real Estate Commission. The Real Estate Licensing Act is the law governing the activities associated with the real estate brokerage profession. The rules and regulations of the Pennsylvania Real Estate Commission are administrative in nature and implement and clarify the statutory law.

The first statutory law regulating the real estate profession was the Real Estate Broker's Licensing Act of 1929. This law was amended many times over the years and finally was replaced by the current law. The current law is substantially similar to the previous law; however, it modernizes and clarifies many of the sections.

The regulations issued under the Real Estate Broker's Licensing Act of 1929 continue to be effective except where they are inconsistent with the new law, in which case the regulation is null and void. The new law has a provision (Section 404) to speed the implementation of new rules and regulations. However, until the new regulations are effective, the state portion of the examination will be based only on the statutory law. That is, even though the old regulations remain effective on an interim basis, the examination will not include questions on them. When new regulations are adopted and published, the examination will again include questions on both the law and on the rules and regulations of the Pennsylvania Real Estate Commission.

This guide is designed to assist the licensure applicant in preparing for the Pennsylvania license law portion of the examination. It is divided into four parts.

In Part I the 1980 statutory law is reproduced in its entirety. The applicant should read the law carefully in order to obtain a general understanding of its organization and content. At the end of Part I there is a summary of the key time limits effective under the new Act.

Part II is a section-by-section analysis of the law. The text of each section is repeated and then that section is explained. Also included in Part II are many exhibits that summarize key provisions of the law. These exhibits should prove helpful in learning the important concepts of the law.

Part III deals with preparing for the examination itself. Included in this section are helpful suggestions on how best to prepare for and take the examination. There are practice questions in the format used in the examination, with answers and a brief explanation of the answer.

Part IV is a complete sample examination and an answer key.

In the appendix are the current rules and regulations of the State Real Estate Commission. Both statutory law and rules and regulations are subject to change. Statutory law changes infrequently. However, the rules and regulations of the Real Estate Commission are constantly undergoing modification. While every effort is being made to ensure that the rules and regulations reproduced here are current, the applicant should check to be certain that no major revision has occurred since the publication of the latest printing of this guide.

Also in the appendix, for your information, is the Code of Ethics of the National Association of Realtors®.

To facilitate the use of the guide, there is also a comprehensive index keyed to the section numbers of the law.

It is gratifying to see both men and women establishing successful careers in real estate. However, to refer to both male and female professionals in this guide as "he/she," "him/her," and "his/her" would be awkward. Therefore, throughout this guide, the masculine personal pronouns and adjectives "he," "him," and "his" will be used to refer to both the male and female real estate professional.

I wish to acknowledge the assistance of Fred Brown of the Pennsylvania Association of Realtors, and Dr. Kenneth M. Lusht, Dr. Ray Watson, and Shirley Hendrick of The Pennsylvania State University for their assistance. I also thank Mary B. Winner for her editorial assistance in the preparation of the manuscript. I especially wish to express my thanks to my wife Susan for her support and encouragement.

Ronald M. Friedman

October 1980

PART I

Text of the Law

The following is the full text of the Real Estate Licensing Act of 1980. It should be read carefully so that the reader will have a general overview of its organization and its key provisions.

REAL ESTATE LICENSING ACT OF 1980

AN ACT

Establishing the State Real Estate Commission and providing for the licensing of real estate brokers and salesmen.

TABLE OF CONTENTS

CHAPTER 1. GENERAL PROVISIONS

Section 101. Short title. This act shall be known and may be cited as the "Real Estate Licensing Act."

CHAPTER 2. DEFINITIONS

Section 201. Definitions. The following words and phrases, when used in this act, shall have, unless the context clearly indicates otherwise, the meanings given to them in this section:

"Associate broker" A broker employed by another broker.

"Broker" Any person who, for another and for a fee, commission or other valuable consideration:

(1) negotiates with or aids any person in locating or obtaining for purchase or lease any real estate;

(2) negotiates the listing, sale, purchase, exchange, lease, financing or option for any real estate;

(3) manages or appraises any real estate;
(4) represents himself as a real estate consultant, counsellor, house finder;
(5) undertakes to promote the sale, exchange, purchase or rental of real estate: provided, however, that this provision shall not include any person whose main business is that of advertising, promotion or public relations; or
(6) attempts to perform any of the above acts.

"Broker of record" A sole proprietor or principal individual broker of a licensed corporation, partnership or association or other entity, foreign or domestic.

"Builder-owner salesperson" Any person who is a full-time employee of a builder-owner of single and multifamily dwellings located within the Commonwealth and as such employee shall be authorized and empowered to list for sale, sell or offer for sale, or to negotiate the sale or exchange of real estate, or to lease or rent, or offer to lease, rent or place for rent, any real estate owned by his builder-owner employer, or collect or offer, or attempt to collect, rent for the use of real estate owned by his builder-owner employer, for and on behalf of such builder-owner employer.

"Commission" The State Real Estate Commission.

"Commissioner" Commissioner of Professional and Occupational Affairs.

"Department" The Department of State acting through the Commissioner of Professional and Occupational Affairs.

"Employ, employed, employee, employment" The use of the words employ, employed, employee or employment in this act shall apply to the relationship of independent contractor as well as to the relationship of employment, except as applied to builder-owner salespersons.

"Limited broker" Any person, partnership, association or corporation engaging in or carrying on the business or act in the capacity of a broker within the Commonwealth exclusively within the limited field or branch of business which applies to cemetery lots, plots and mausoleum spaces or openings.

"Limited salesperson" Any person employed by a broker or limited broker to perform duties as defined hereinunder limited broker. No person employed by a broker to perform duties other than those activities as defined hereinunder limited broker shall be required to be licensed as a limited salesperson.

"Person" Any individual, corporation, partnership, association or other entity foreign or domestic.

"Real estate" Any interest or estate in land, whether corporeal, incorporeal, freehold or nonfreehold, whether the land is situated in this Commonwealth or elsewhere including leasehold interests.

"Rental listing referral agent" Any person who owns or manages a business which collects rental information for the purpose of referring prospective tenants to rental units or locations of such units. The term "rental listing referral agent" shall not include any employee or official of any public housing authority created pursuant to the State or Federal law.

"Salesperson" Any person employed by a licensed real estate broker to list for sale, sell or offer for sale, to buy or offer to buy or to negotiate the purchase or sale or exchange of real estate or to negotiate a loan on real estate or to lease or rent or offer to lease, rent or place for rent any real estate or collect or offer or attempt to collect rent for the use of real estate for or in behalf of such real estate broker. No person employed by a broker to perform duties other than those activities as defined herein under "broker" shall be required to be licensed as a salesperson.

"School" Any person, corporation, partnership, association or other entity, foreign or domestic, which conducts classes in real estate subjects, but which is not a college or university duly accredited by the Middle States Association of Colleges and Secondary Schools or equivalent accreditation.

CHAPTER 3. APPLICATION OF THE ACT AND PENALTIES

Section 301. Unlawful to conduct business without license. From and after the effective date of this act, it shall be unlawful for any person, directly or indirectly, to engage in or conduct, or to advertise or hold himself out as engaging in or conducting the business, or acting in the capacity of a broker or salesperson, limited broker, limited salesperson, builder-owner salesperson, or rental listing referral agent within this Commonwealth without first being licensed as such as provided in this act, unless he is exempted from obtaining a license under the provisions of section 304.

Section 302. Civil suits. No action or suit shall be instituted, nor recovery be had, in any court of this Commonwealth by any person for compensation for any act done or service rendered, the doing or rendering of which is prohibited under the provisions of this act by a person other than a licensed broker, salesperson, limited broker, limited salesperson, builder-owner salesperson or rental listing referral agent, unless such person was duly licensed and registered hereunder as broker or salesperson at the time of offering to perform any such act or service or procuring any promise or contract for the payment of compensation for any such contemplated act or service.

Section 303. Criminal penalties. Any person who shall, after the effective date of this act, engage in or carry on the business, or act in the capacity of a broker, salesperson, limited broker, limited salesperson, builder-owner salesperson or rental listing referral agent, within this Commonwealth, without a license, or shall carry on or continue business after the suspension or revocation of any such license issued to him, or shall employ any person as a salesperson or limited salesperson to whom a license has not been issued, or whose license as such shall have been revoked or suspended, shall be guilty of a summary offense and upon conviction thereof for a first offense shall be sentenced to pay a fine not exceeding $500 or suffer imprisonment, not exceeding three months, or both and for a second or subsequent offense shall be guilty of a felony of the third degree and upon conviction thereof, shall be sentenced to pay a fine of not less than $2,000 but not more than $5,000 or to imprisonment for not less than one year but not more than two years, or both.

Section 304. Exclusions. The provisions of this act shall not apply to an owner of real estate with respect to property owned or leased by such owner, provided that in the case of a partnership or corporation, this exclusion shall not extend to more than five of its partners or officers, respectively, but to no other partnership or corporation personnel or employee except the employees of a public utility acting in the ordinary course of utility related business under the provisions of Title 66 of the Pennsylvania Consolidated Statutes (relating to public utilities), with respect to negotiating the purchase, sale or lease of property nor shall this act be construed to include in any way the services rendered by an attorney in fact under a duly executed and recorded power of attorney from the owner or lessor (provided such power of attorney is not utilized to circumvent the intent of this act); nor an attorney at law, nor shall it be held to include a person acting as receiver, trustee in bankruptcy, administrator, executor, trustee, guardian or while acting under a court order or under the authority of a will or of a trust instrument, nor shall this act apply to the duly elected officer of any banking institution or trust company operating under Federal or State banking laws where real estate of the banking institution or trust company only is involved, nor shall they be held to include any officer or employee of a cemetery company who, as incidental to his principal duties and without remuneration therefor, shows lots in such company's cemetery to persons for their use as a family burial lot, and who accepts deposits on such lots for the representatives of the cemetery company, legally authorized to sell the same, nor shall it be held to include any properly licensed auctioneer, under statutes of this State, while performing authorized duties at any bona fide auction.

CHAPTER 4. POWERS AND DUTIES OF THE STATE REAL ESTATE COMMISSION – GENERAL

Section 401. Duty to issue licenses. It shall be the duty of the department to issue licenses to individuals, copartnerships and corporations, who shall comply with the provisions of this act.

Section 402. Approval of schools. Any school which shall offer or conduct any course or courses of study in real estate shall first obtain approval from, and thereafter abide by the rules and regulations of the commission covering such schools.

Section 403. Authority to examine applicants. The commission is empowered to prescribe the subjects to be tested. The department shall arrange for the services of professional testing services to write and administer examinations on behalf of the commission in accordance with commission guidance and approval.

Section 404. Power to promulgate regulations.

(a) The commission shall have the power to promulgate rules or regulations in order to administer and effectuate the purposes of this act. All existing rules or regulations adopted pursuant to the act of May 1, 1929 (P.L. 1216, No. 427), known as the "Real Estate Brokers License Act of one thousand nine hundred and twenty nine," shall remain in full force and effect until modified by the commission. The proposed rules and regulations shall be submitted to the Secretary of the Senate and the Chief Clerk of the House of Representatives who shall cause the rules or regulations to be printed and distributed among all members of both chambers in the same manner as a reorganization plan. If both bodies fail to act within 60 days of receipt of such rules or regulations, or within ten legislative days after receipt, whichever shall last occur, rules or regulations adopted by the commission shall be promulgated pursuant to the provisions of the act of July 31, 1968 (P.L. 769, No. 240), referred to as the Commonwealth Documents Law and 45 Pa.C.S. Part II (relating to publication and effectiveness of Commonwealth documents).

(b) If either chamber disapproves any rule or regulation, such information shall be certified by the Speaker of the House of Representatives or President pro tempore of the Senate to the commission, any such rule or regulation shall not be promulgated as a final rule or regulation.

Section 405. Duty to keep records confidential. Neither the Commissioner of Professional and Occupational Affairs, any member of the commission, nor any deputy, secretary, representative, clerk or other employee of the Commonwealth, shall directly or indirectly, willfully, exhibit, publish, divulge, or make known to any person or persons any record, report, statement, letter, or any other matter, fact or thing except in accordance with the laws of this Commonwealth dealing with the public's right to access to Commonwealth proceedings and records. A person violating the provisions of this section shall be guilty of a misdemeanor and sentenced to pay a fine not exceeding $1,000: Provided, however, that the provisions of this section shall not apply to any ruling or decision of the commission, with the record relative thereto, and upon which the same was founded, which ruling or decision shall have been duly made and entered under and in accordance with the provisions of this act, after investigation and hearing as hereinafter provided. All such records shall, immediately upon the entry of such ruling or decision, become public records of the department, subject to inspection by any person interested.

Section 406. Administration and enforcement. The commission shall have the power and its duty shall be to administer and enforce the laws of the Commonwealth relating to those activities involving real estate for which licensing is required under this act and to instruct and require its agents to bring prosecutions for unauthorized and unlawful practice.

CHAPTER 5. QUALIFICATIONS AND APPLICATIONS FOR LICENSES

Subchapter A. General

Section 501. Reputation; inactive licensee.

(a) Licenses shall be granted only to persons who bear a good reputation for honesty, trustworthiness, integrity and competence to transact the business of broker, salesperson, limited broker, limited salesperson, builder-owner salesperson or rental listing referral agent, in such manner as to safeguard the interest of the public, and only after satisfactory proof of such has been presented to the commission as it shall by regulation require.

(b) Any person who remains inactive for a period of five years without renewing his licenses shall, prior to having a license reissued to him, submit to and pass an examination.

Subchapter B. Broker's License

Section 511. Qualifications for license. The applicant for a broker's license, shall as a condition precedent to obtaining a license, take the broker's license examination and score a passing grade. Prior to taking the examination:

(1) The applicant shall be at least 21 years of age.
(2) The applicant shall be a high school graduate or shall produce proof satisfactory to the commission of an education equivalent thereto.
(3) The applicant shall have completed 16 semester credit hours of 15 hours each in real estate instruction in areas of study prescribed by the rules of the commission.
(4) The applicant shall have been engaged full time as a sales person for at least three years or possess educational or experience qualifications which the commission deems to be the equivalent thereof.

Section 512. Application for license.

(a) An application for a license as real estate broker shall be made in writing, to the department, upon a form provided for the purpose by the department and shall contain such information as to the applicant as the commission shall require.

(b) The application shall be accompanied by two photographs of the applicant or in the case of a copartnership, association or corporation of the applicant members or officers thereof.

(c) The application shall state the place of business for which such license is desired.

(d) The application shall be received by the commission within three years of the date upon which the applicant took the examination.

Section 513. Corporations, partnerships and associations. If the applicant for a broker's license is a corporation, partnership or association, then the provisions of Sections 511 and 512 shall apply to the individual designated as broker of record. The employees of said corporation, partnership or association actually engaging in or intending to engage in the real estate business shall meet the provisions of Sections 512 and 522.

Subchapter C. Salesperson's License

Section 521. Qualifications for license. Each applicant shall as a condition precedent to obtaining a license, take the salesperson license examination and score a passing grade. Prior to taking the examination:

(1) The applicant shall be at least 18 years of age.
(2) The applicant shall have completed four semester credit hours of 15 hours each in real estate instruction in areas of study prescribed by the rules of the commission.

Section 522. Application for license.

(a) An application for a license as salesperson shall be made, in writing to the department, upon a form provided for the purpose by the department, and shall contain such information as to the applicant, as the commission shall require.

(b) The applicant shall submit a sworn statement by the broker with whom he desires to be affiliated certifying that the broker will actively supervise and train the applicant.

(c) The application shall be received by the commission within three years of the date upon which the applicant took the examination.

Subchapter D. Limited Broker's License

Section 531. Qualifications for license. Each applicant for a limited broker's license shall as a condition to obtaining a license take the limited broker's license examination and score a passing grade. Prior to taking the examination:

(1) The applicant shall be at least 21 years of age.
(2) The applicant shall have been engaged full time as a salesperson or limited salesperson for at least three years or possess educational or experience qualifications which the commission deems to be the equivalent thereof.

Section 532. Application for license.

(a) An application for a license as a limited broker shall be made, in writing, to the department, upon a form provided for the purpose by the department and shall contain such information as to the applicant, as the commission shall require.

(b) The applicant shall have completed four semester credit hours of 15 hours each in real estate instruction in areas of study prescribed by the rules of the commission.

(c) The application shall be received by the commission within three years of the date upon which the applicant took the examination.

Section 533. Corporations, partnerships, associations or other entities. If the applicant for a limited broker's license is a corporation, partnership, association, or other entity, foreign or domestic, then the provisions of Sections 531 and 532 shall apply to the individual designated as Broker of Record, as well as those members actually engaging in or intending to engage in the real estate business.

Subchapter E. Limited Salesperson's License

Section 541. Qualifications for license. The applicant for a limited salesperson's license shall be at least 18 years of age.

Section 542. Application for license.

(a) An application for a license as a limited salesperson shall be made, in writing, to the department, upon a form provided for the purpose by the department, and shall contain such information as to the applicant, as the commission shall require.

(b) The applicant for a license shall submit a sworn affidavit by the broker or limited broker with whom he desires to be affiliated certifying that the broker will actively supervise and train the applicant and certifying the truth and accuracy of the certification of the applicant.

Subchapter F. Builder-Owner Salesperson's License

Section 551. Qualifications for license. Each applicant for a builder-owner salesperson's license, shall as a condition precedent to obtaining a license, take the standard real estate salesperson's license examination and score a passing grade. Prior to taking the examination:

(1) The applicant shall be 18 years of age.
(2) The applicant shall be employed by a builder-owner possessing those qualifications as contained in Section 501.

Section 552. Application for license.

(a) An application for a license as a builder-owner salesperson shall be made, in writing to the department, upon a form provided for the purpose by the department, and shall contain such information as to the applicant as the commission shall require.

(b) The applicant shall submit a sworn statement by the builder-owner by whom he is employed certifying to such employment.

(c) The application shall be received by the commission within three years of the date upon which the applicant took the examination.

Subchapter G. Rental Listing Referral Agent's License

Section 561. Qualifications for license. The qualification for licensure as a rental listing referral agent shall be the same as those set forth in Sections 521 and 522 except that the applicant need not be affiliated with a broker.

CHAPTER 6. DUTIES OF LICENSEES

Section 601. Duty of brokers and limited brokers to maintain office.

(a) Each resident licensed broker (which term in this section shall include limited broker) shall maintain a fixed office within this Commonwealth. The original license of a broker and of each licensee employed by such broker shall be prominently displayed in an office of the broker. The address of the office shall be designated on the current renewal form. In case of removal of a broker's office from the designated location, all licensees registered at that location shall make application to the commission before such removal or within ten days thereafter, designating the new location of the office, and shall pay the required fees, whereupon the commission shall issue a renewal form at the new location for the unexpired period, if the new location complies with the terms of this act. Each licensed broker shall maintain a sign on the outside of his office indicating the proper licensed brokerage name.

(b) If the applicant for a broker's license intends to maintain more than one place of business within the Commonwealth, he shall apply for and obtain an additional license in his name at each branch office. Every such application shall state the location of such branch office. Effective 24 months after the effective date of this act, each branch office shall be under the direction and supervision of a manager who is either the broker of record or an associate broker: provided, however, that such broker of record or an associate broker may direct and supervise more than one branch office.

Section 602. Nonresident licensees.

(a) A nonresident of this Commonwealth may be licensed as a broker or a salesperson, upon complying with all provisions and conditions as promulgated by the commission.

(b) In connection with the application of a nonresident of this Commonwealth for a license as broker or salesperson, the commission may accept, in lieu of the recommendations and statements otherwise required to accompany the application for such licensure, the license as broker or salesperson issued to such applicant by the proper authority of the state of his licensure. In such case the licensee need not maintain a place of business within this Commonwealth. It is hereby expressly stipulated, that the provisions of this subsection shall apply to licensed brokers and salespersons of those states under the laws of which similar recognition and courtesies are extended to licensed brokers and salespersons of this Commonwealth.

Section 603. Employment of associate brokers, salespersons. No associate broker or salesperson (which term in this section shall include limited salesperson) shall be employed by any other broker than is designated upon the renewal form issued to said associate broker or said salesperson. Whenever a licensed salesperson or associate broker desires to change his employment from one licensed broker to another, he shall notify the commission in writing at least ten days prior to the intended date of change, pay the required fee, and return his current renewal license. The commission, shall, upon receipt of acknowledgement from the new broker, of the change of employment forthwith issue a new renewal form and pocket card, but in the interim at such time as the change in affiliation of the salesperson or associate broker occurs, he shall maintain a copy of the notification sent to the commissioner as his temporary license pending receipt of his renewal form. It shall be the duty of the applicant to notify the commission if a new renewal form or other pertinent communication is not received from the commission within 30 days.

Section 604. Prohibited acts. The commission may upon its own motion, and shall promptly upon the verified complaint in writing of any person setting forth a complaint under this section, ascertain the facts and, if warranted, hold a hearing for the suspension or revocation of a license or for the imposition of fines not exceeding $500. The commission shall have power to refuse a license for cause or to suspend or revoke a license or to levy fines up to $500 where the said license has been obtained by false representation, or by fraudulent act or conduct, or where a licensee, in performing or attempting to perform any of the acts mentioned herein, is found guilty of:

(1) Making any substantial misrepresentation.

(2) Making any false promise of a character likely to influence, persuade or induce any person to enter into any contract or agreement when he could not or did not intend to keep such promise.

(3) Pursuing a continued and flagrant course of misrepresentation or making of false promises through salesperson, associate broker, other persons, or any medium of advertising, or otherwise.

(4) Any misleading or untruthful advertising, or using any other trade name or insignia or membership in any real estate association or organization, of which the licensee is not a member.

(5) Failure to comply with the following requirements:

(i) all deposits or other moneys accepted by every person, holding a real estate broker license under the provisions of this act, shall be retained by such real estate broker pending consummation or termination of the transaction involved, and shall be accounted for in the full amount thereof at the time of the consummation or termination;

(ii) every salesperson and associate broker promptly on receipt by him of a deposit or other moneys on any transaction in which he is engaged on behalf of his broker-employer, shall pay over the deposit to the broker;

(iii) a broker shall not commingle the money or other property of his principal with his own;

(iv) every broker shall immediately deposit such moneys, of whatever kind or nature, belonging to others, in a separate custodial or trust fund account maintained by the broker with some bank or recognized depository until the transaction involved is consummated or terminated, at which time the broker shall account for the full amount received. Under no circumstances shall a broker permit any advance payment of funds belonging to others to be deposited in the broker's business or personal account, or to be commingled with any funds he may have on deposit; or

(v) every broker shall keep records of all funds deposited therein, which records shall indicate clearly the date and from whom he received money, the date deposited, the dates of withdrawals, and other pertinent information concerning the transaction, and shall show clearly for whose account the money is deposited and to whom the money belongs. All such records and funds shall be subject to inspection by the commission. Such separate custodial or trust fund account shall designate the broker, as trustee, and such account must provide for withdrawal of funds without previous notice. All such records shall be available to the commission, or its representatives, immediately after proper demand or after written notice given, or upon written notice given to the depository.

(6) Failing to preserve for three years following its consummation records relating to any real estate transaction.

(7) Acting for more than one party in a transaction without the knowledge and consent in writing of all parties for whom he acts.

(8) Placing a "for sale" or "for rent" sign on any property without the written consent of the owner, or his authorized agent.

(9) Failing to voluntarily furnish a copy of any listing, sale, lease, or other contract relevant to a real estate transaction to all signatories thereof at the time of execution.

(10) Failing to specify a definite termination date that is not subject to prior notice, in any listing contract.

(11) Inducing any party to a contract, sale or lease to break such contract for the purpose of substitution in lieu thereof of a new contract, where such substitution is motivated by the personal gain of the licensee.

(12) Accepting a commission or any valuable consideration by a salesperson or associate broker for the performance of any acts specified in this act, from any person, except the licensed real estate broker with whom he is affiliated.

(13) Failing to disclose to an owner in writing his intention or true position if he directly or indirectly through a third party, purchased for himself or acquires or intends to acquire any interest in or any option to purchase property which has been listed with his office to sell or lease.

(14) Being convicted in a court of competent jurisdiction of this or any other state, or Federal court, of forgery, embezzlement, obtaining money under false pretenses, bribery, larceny, extortion, conspiracy to defraud, or any similar offense or offenses, or pleading guilty or nolo contendere to any such offense or offenses.

(15) Violating any rule or regulation promulgated by the commission in the interest of the public and consistent with the provisions of this act.

(16) In the case of a broker licensee, failing to exercise adequate supervision over the activities of his licensed salespersons or associate brokers within the scope of this act.

(17) Failing, within a reasonable time as defined by the commission, to provide information requested by the commission as the result of a formal or informal complaint to the commission, which would indicate a violation of this act.

(18) Soliciting, selling or offering for sale real property by offering free lots, or conducting lotteries or contests or offering prizes for the purpose of influencing by deceptive conduct any purchaser or prospective purchaser of real property. The commission shall promulgate necessary rules and regulations to provide standards for nondeception conduct under this paragraph.

(19) Paying or accepting, giving or charging any undisclosed commission, rebate, compensation or profit or expenditures for a principal, or in violation of this act.

(20) Any conduct in a real estate transaction which demonstrates bad faith, dishonesty, untrustworthiness, or incompetency.

(21) Performing any act for which an appropriate real estate license is required and is not currently in effect.

(22) Violating any provision of the Act of October 27, 1955 (P.L. 744, No. 222), known as the "Pennsylvania Human Relations Act," or any order or consent decree of the Pennsylvania Human Relations Commission issued pursuant to such act if such order or consent decree resulted from a complaint of discrimination in the area of activities authorized by virtue of this act. Such activities include but are not limited to:

  (i) Accepting listings on the understanding that illegal discrimination in the sale or rental of housing is to be practiced due to race, color, religious creed, sex, ancestry, national origin, physical handicap, disability, or use of a guide dog because of blindness of user of a prospective lessee or purchaser.

  (ii) Giving false information for purposes of discrimination in the rental or sale of housing due to race, color, religious creed, sex, ancestry, national origin, physical handicap, disability, or use of a guide dog because of blindness of user of a prospective lessee or purchaser.

(iii) Making distinctions in locations of housing or dates of availability of housing for purposes of discrimination in the rental or sale of such housing due to race, color, religious creed, sex, ancestry, national origin, physical handicap, disability, or use of a guide dog because of blindness of user of the prospective lessee or purchaser.

Nothing contained in paragraph (22) is intended to preclude the State Real Estate Commission from conducting its own investigation and maintaining its own file on any complaint of discrimination. The intent hereunder is to allow the Pennsylvania Human Relations Commission a reasonable period of time to conduct its own investigations, hold hearings, render its decisions and inform the Pennsylvania Real Estate Commission of its findings prior to the State Real Estate Commission taking action against any broker, salesperson or sales associate charged with a violation of paragraph (22).

If in the event the Pennsylvania Human Relations Commission does not act on a discrimination complaint within 90 days after it is filed with the Pennsylvania Human Relations Commission then the State Real Estate Commission may proceed with action against such licensee.

The 90-day waiting period delaying State Real Estate Commission action against licensee accused of discrimination applies only in initial complaints against such licensee, second or subsequent complaints may be brought by individuals or the Pennsylvania Human Relations Commission directly to the State Real Estate Commission.

Section 605. Out-of-state land sales — approval. Any person who proposes to engage in sales of a promotional nature in this Commonwealth for a property located outside of this Commonwealth, shall first apply to the commission for its approval before so doing, and they and their salesmen shall comply with such rules, regulations, restrictions and conditions pertaining thereto as the commission may impose as well as all those provisions set forth in this act.

CHAPTER 7. PROCEEDINGS BEFORE THE COMMISSION

Section 701. Hearings held by commission.

(a) The said hearings may be held by the commission or any members thereof, or by any of its duly authorized representatives, or by any other person duly authorized by the commission for such purpose in any particular case.

(b) The commission may adopt the findings in the report or may, with or without additional testimony, either return the matter to the representative for such further consideration as the commission deems necessary or make additional or other findings of fact on the basis of all the legally probative evidence in the record and enter its conclusions of law and order in accordance with the requirements for the issuance of an adjudication under 2 Pa.C.S. §103, known as the Administrative Agency Law.

(c) Proceedings before the commission shall be conducted in accordance with Title 1, Part 2 of the Pennsylvania Code.

Section 702. Imputed knowledge, limitations. No violation of any of the provisions of this act on the part of any salesperson, associate broker, or other employee of any licensed broker, shall be grounds for the revocation or suspension of the license of the employer of such salesperson, associate broker, or employee, unless it shall appear upon the hearings held, that such employer had actual knowledge of such violation. A course of dealing shown to have been followed by such employee shall constitute prima facie evidence of such knowledge upon the part of his employer.

CHAPTER 8. REAL ESTATE RECOVERY FUND

Section 801. Establishment of the fund. There is hereby established the Real Estate Recovery Fund for the purposes hereinafter set forth in this act.

Section 802. Funding of the fund. Each licensee entitled to renew his license on or after February 28, 1980, shall, when so renewing his license pay in addition to the applicable license fee a further fee of $10, which shall be paid and credited to the Real Estate Recovery Fund, thereafter any person upon receiving his initial real estate license, shall, in addition to all fees, pay into the Real Estate Recovery Fund a sum of $10. If at the commencement of any biennial renewal period beginning in 1982 and thereafter, the balance of the fund is less than $300,000, the commission may assess an additional fee, in addition to the renewal fee, against each licensee in an amount not to exceed $10 which will yield revenues sufficient to bring the balance of the fund to $500,000. All said fees shall be paid into the State Treasury and credited to the Real Estate Recovery Fund, and said deposits shall be allocated solely for the purposes of the fund as provided in this act. The fund shall be invested and interest/dividends shall accrue to the fund.

Section 803. Application for recovery from fund.

(a) When any aggrieved person obtains a final judgment in any court of competent jurisdiction against any person licensed under this act, upon grounds of fraud, misrepresentation or deceit with reference to any transaction for which a license is required under this act and which cause of action occurred on or after the effective date of this act, the aggrieved person may, upon termination of all proceedings, including reviews and appeals, file an application in the court in which the judgment was entered for an order directing payment out of the Real Estate Recovery Fund of the amount unpaid upon the judgment.

(b) The aggrieved person shall be required to show:

(1) That he is not a spouse of the debtor; or the personal respresentative of said spouse.

(2) That he has obtained a final judgment as set out in this section.

(3) That all reasonable personal acts, rights of discovery and such other remedies at law and in equity as exist have been exhausted in the collection thereof.

(4) That he is making said application no more than one year after the termination of the proceedings, including reviews and appeals in connection with the judgment.

(c) The commission shall have the right to answer actions provided for under this section, and subject to court approval, it may compromise a claim based upon the application of the aggrieved party.

(d) When there is an order of the court to make payment or a claim is otherwise to be levied against the fund, such amount shall be paid to the claimant in accordance with the limitations contained in this section. Notwithstanding any other provisions of this section, the liability of that portion of the fund allocated for the purpose of this act shall not exceed $20,000 for any one judgment. If the $20,000 liability of the Real Estate Recovery Fund as provided herein is insufficient to pay in full claims adjudicated valid of all aggrieved persons against any one licensee, such $20,000 shall be distributed among them in such ratio that the respective claims of the aggrieved applicants bear to the aggregate of such claims held valid. If, at any time, the money deposited in the Real Estate Recovery Fund is insufficient to satisfy any duly authorized claim or portion thereof, the commission shall, when sufficient money has been deposited in the fund, satisfy such unpaid claims or portions thereof, in the order that such claims or portions thereof were originally filed, plus accumulated interest at the rate of 6% a year.

(e) Upon petition of the commission the court may require all claimants and prospective claimants against one licensee to be joined in one action, to the end that the respective rights of all such claimants to the Real Estate Recovery Fund may be equitably adjudicated and settled.

(f) Should the commission pay from the Real Estate Recovery Fund any amount in settlement of a claim as provided for in this act against a licensee, the license of that person shall automatically suspend upon the effective date of the payment thereof by the commission. No such licensee shall be granted reinstatement until he has repaid in full plus interest at the rate of 6% a year, the amount paid from the Real Estate Recovery Fund.

CHAPTER 9. REPEALER AND EFFECTIVE DATE

Section 901. Repealer. The act of May 1, 1929 (P.L. 1216, No. 427), known as the "Real Estate Brokers License Act of one thousand nine hundred and twenty-nine," is repealed to the following conditions:

(1) All valid licenses issued prior to the effective date of this act under the provisions of said 1929 Act shall continue with full force and validity during the period for which issued. For the subsequent license period, and each license period thereafter, the commission shall renew such licenses without requiring any license examination to be taken: provided, however, that applicants for renewal or holders of such licenses shall be subject to all other provisions of this act.

(2) All proceedings in progress on the effective date shall continue to proceed under the terms of the act under which they were brought.

(3) All offenses alleged to have occurred prior to the effective date of this act shall be processed under the act of May 1, 1929 (P.L. 1216, No. 427).

Section 902. Effective date. Section 561 shall take effect September 1, 1980 and the remaining provisions of this act shall take effect immediately.

Exhibit 1
SUMMARY OF TIME LIMITS

• Imprisonment for conviction of violation of licensing law, first offense [§303]	Not exceeding 3 months
• Imprisonment for conviction of violation of licensing law, second offense [§303]	1 to 2 years
• Time lapse after which a person who remains inactive without renewing his or her license must resubmit an application and pass an examination [§501(b)]	5 years
• Minimum age of broker and limited broker [§§511(1), 513(1)]	21 years
• Length of time an applicant for broker or limited broker's license to have been engaged as a full-time salesperson or limited salesperson [§511(4)]	3 years
• Time within which an applicant must submit an application for licensure after having taken the examination [§§512(d), 522(c), 532(c)]	3 years
• Minimum age salesperson, limited salesperson, builder-owner salesperson, rental listing referral agent [§§521(1), 551(1), 561]	18 years
• Prior notice to the Commission of a licensee's removal from a designated location to another [§601(a)]	10 days
• Notice to the Commission by a licensee that the licensee intends to change employers [§603]	10 days prior to the change
• Notification to the Commission by a licensee that a renewal form other communication has not been received [§603]	If not received within 30 days
• Salesperson or associate broker to pay over to broker deposits received from others [§604(5)(ii)]	Promptly
• Broker to deposit monies in trust or custodial account after receipt [§604(5)(iv)]	Immediately
• Length of time following termination of a transaction for which a licensee must preserve records of the transaction [§604(6)]	3 years
• After a complaint of illegal discrimination filed with the Pennsylvania Human Relations Commission, time lapse before the Real Estate Commission may proceed against a licensee [§604(22)]	90 days
• Time within which a claim from the Real Estate Discovery Fund must be made following termination of legal proceedings against a licensee [§803(b)(4)]	1 year

PART II

Analysis of the Law

CHAPTER 1.
GENERAL PROVISIONS

Section 101. Short title. This act shall be known and may be cited as the "Real Estate Licensing Act."

Section 101 merely names the law. It is the Real Estate Licensing Act of 1980, and all official citations to the law will use this name. Sometimes, the law will be cited by reference to its location in the compilation of Pennsylvania's statutes. The 1929 Act was found in Chapter 63 Sections 431 through 448, *Purdon's Pennsylvania Statutes Annotated,* although the new law has not been assigned section numbers in Chapter 63 and it is possible that the section numbers will vary from the former law. It is not necessary to know the chapter and section numbers for examination purposes, nor is it necessary to know whether a provision is part of the statutory law or whether it is in rules and regulations of the Real Estate Commission. However, it is necessary to know the content of the law and the rules and regulations.

CHAPTER 2.
DEFINITIONS

Section 201. Definitions. The following words and phrases, when used in this act, shall have, unless the context clearly indicates otherwise, the meanings given to them in this section.

This definition chapter is important because it establishes the meanings for terms used in the law. Note that for purposes of definition within the context of the law, a word or phrase may have a different meaning than that word or phrase may have when it is used in everyday conversation. For example, the law defines "employee" as including "independent contractors." Generally, independent contractors are self-employed individuals who work on a contract basis for another. The persons for whom independent contractors perform services are technically not employers and are not required by federal law to withhold income taxes or contribute to social security payments. Examples of independent contractors are babysitters, day workers, and many real estate salespersons and associate brokers. However, for purposes of the real estate licensing law "independent contractors" are considered to be "employees" and all references in the law to employees includes those who are technically independent contractors.

The law defines the word "school" as those who conduct classes in real estate subjects. This definition is only for purposes of the law, and it would be unreasonable to give the word "school" such a meaning in everyday conversation.

Note also that it is possible for a word specifically defined in the law to have a different meaning within the law. However, any such variance would arise only when the context in which the word is used clearly indicates a different meaning of that word.

"Associate broker." A broker employed by another broker.

The term associate broker refers to a person who is a licensed broker but who is not a sole practitioner and is associated with another licensed broker. The law defines "associate broker" as being in the employ of another licensed broker. The law requires that one broker be designated as "broker of record" and that only one broker be responsible for supervising the employees and be ultimately responsible for complying with all laws, rules, and regulations. In situations where two licensed brokers are partners in a real estate brokerage business, only one may be designated as "broker of record." The other will be the "associate broker" and, for purposes of the law, will be considered to be in the employ of the broker of record. Remember that an associate broker has all of the rights and duties of a broker of record. However, for purposes of the law, he is not designated as being the broker directly responsible to the Real Estate Commission for the operation of the real estate business.

> "Broker." Any person who, for another and for a fee, commission or other valuable consideration:
>
> (1) negotiates with or aids any person in locating or obtaining for purchase or lease any real estate;
> (2) negotiates the listing, sale, purchase, exchange, lease, financing or option for any real estate;
> (3) manages or appraises any real estate;
> (4) represents himself as a real estate consultant, counsellor, house finder;
> (5) undertakes to promote the sale, exchange, purchase or rental of real estate: provided, however that this provision shall not include any person whose main business is that of advertising, promotion of public relations; or
> (6) attempts to perform any of the above acts.

The definition of "broker" is very important because it lists the activities which may bring a person within the requirements of the law. Note that in order to be considered to be a broker the person must perform these activities:

- For another,
- For a fee, commission, or other valuable consideration.

Therefore a person who performs these activities on his own behalf is not within the definition of "broker." And a person who performs these activities for another but is not paid money or other consideration also is not within the definition of "broker." "Valuable consideration" other than money would be property or services given by one person to another in exchange for the activities listed in the definition. For example, if a person were to negotiate the sale of property for another and the other were to give that person an airline ticket to Florida in exchange, this would be valuable consideration within the meaning of the law, even though no money changed hands. Remember, if *anything* of value passes into the hands of the person performing the services for another, then there is presumed to be consideration and the person performing the services would come within the licensing law's definition of a "broker." This is so even though the property or services exchanged is minimal.

The law continues enumerating the activities which, if performed for another for consideration, bring a person within the statutory definition of broker. Note that the activities include those not traditionally associated with real estate brokerage. Among the activities of this type are the arranging for financing of the purchase, exchange, sale, or lease of real property, and activities as a real estate consultant or counselor.

The law specifically excludes persons whose primary business is advertising and promoting public relations. This would exempt newspapers and other advertising media which advertise or promote real property for others.

The law refers to activities performed which involve "any real estate." Under the statutory definition of "real estate," interests in real estate inside the Commonwealth of Pennsylvania as well as interests in other states or other countries would be included. Therefore, if a person within Pennsylvania were to sell or offer for sale real property of another for consideration, for example, building lots in the Bahamas, he would come within the statutory definition of broker. *The test would be whether the enumerated activities took place within the Commonwealth, not where the land or real property interest is located.* However, it should be noted that if the land were located in Pennsylvania and any of the enumerated activities take place outside the commonwealth, it is still necessary for the person performing the activities for another for consideration to be licensed under the Pennsylvania law.

The activities listed in the definition do not actually have to be completed. The activities need only be attempted. Therefore, a person would come within the definition of "broker" if he attempts to appraise property for another for consideration even though he does not complete the task and is not actually paid for the appraisal. Merely attempting to do one of the enumerated activities is enough.

Exhibit 2 summarizes the statutory definition of "broker."

Exhibit 2
DEFINITION OF A "BROKER"

A *broker* is a person who
- For another person,
- For a
  - Fee, or
  - Commission, or
  - Valuable consideration

Does *any* of the following:
- Negotiates with or aids any person in locating or obtaining for purchase or lease any real estate, or
- Negotiates the
  - Listing,
  - Sale,
  - Purchase,
  - Exchange,
  - Lease,
  - Financing,
  - Option,

  for any real estate, or
- Manages or appraises any real estate, or
- Represents himself as a
  - Real estate consultant,
  - Counsellor, or
  - Housefinder,

  or
- Attempts to perform any of the above acts.

"Broker of record." A sole proprietor or principal individual broker of a licensed corporation, partnership or association or other entity, foreign or domestic.

This section defines the licensed broker who is designated as the broker responsible for the real estate business. It may be a sole practitioner, or it may be the broker designated by a corporation or partnership to act as the broker responsible to the Real Estate Commission for the activities of the real estate business. An associate broker would never be considered the broker of record because, by definition, the "associate broker" is in the employ of another broker, who under most circumstances would be the broker of record.

"Builder-owner salesperson." Any person who is a full-time employee of a builder-owner of single and multifamily dwellings located within the Commonwealth and as such employee shall be authorized and empowered to list for sale, sell or offer for sale, or to negotiate the sale or exchange of real estate, or to lease or rent, or offer to lease, rent or place for rent, any real estate owned by his builder-owner employer, or collect or offer, or attempt to collect, rent for the use of real estate owned by his builder-owner employer, for and on behalf of such builder-owner employer.

Under this definition, a person who is in the full-time employ of a builder-owner of single- and multifamily dwellings can engage in some of the activities normally limited to licensed brokers. Note however that the person must be in the *full-time* employ of the person who is actually building the improvements and that the definition only applies to single- and multifamily *dwellings*. Therefore, a salesperson employed by a builder-owner of commercial property would not come within the definition of builder-owner salesperson. The services performed by the builder-owner salesperson are limited to those services listed in the Act which are performed *only* for the builder-owner.

Exhibit 3 summarizes the definition of builder-owner salesperson and the activities in which he may engage.

Exhibit 3
DEFINITION OF A "BUILDER-OWNER SALESPERSON"

A *builder-owner salesperson* is any person who
- Is a full time employee of
- A builder-owner of
  Single-family dwellings and
  Multifamily dwellings
  in Pennsylvania, and

Shall be authorized to
- List for sale,
- Sell or offer for sale,
- Negotiate the sale or exchange,
- Lease or rent,
- Offer to lease,
- Rent or place for rent,
- Collect rent for use of, and
- Attempt to collect rent for use of

Real estate owned by the builder-owner.

A builder-owner salesperson *cannot* purchase, offer to purchase, or advertise to purchase real property interests on behalf of the builder-owner, unless the builder-owner salesperson is duly authorized under a recorded power of attorney or is engaging in these purchase activities for no fee or remuneration. For example, the builder-owner wishes to purchase a tract of land for future development. He sends his full-time employee builder-owner salesperson to inspect a prospective location and gives the salesperson authority to offer the owner $50,000 as a purchase price. This would be a violation of the licensing law. Even though the purchase of property for another has been authorized by the builder-owner and is within the scope of the salesperson's authority, the builder-owner salesperson is not authorized by the licensing law to engage in this activity. The purchase of property for another for a fee or remuneration is limited to brokers. The builder-owner salesperson cannot engage in any of the other activities enumerated in the definition of "broker" in Section 201 except those specifically authorized and listed above.

"Commission." The State Real Estate Commission.

"Commissioner." Commissioner of Professional and Occupational Affairs.

"Department." The Department of State acting through the Commissioner of Professional and Occupational Affairs.

These definitions clarify the names of the parties referred to in the administrative portion of the licensing law. The Real Estate Commission is under the control of the Department of State's Commissioner of Professional and Occupational Affairs.

"Employ, employed, employee, employment." The use of the words employ, employed, employee or employment in this act shall apply to the relationship of independent contractor as well as to the relationship of employment, except as applied to builder-owner salespersons.

Under the common-law definition of "independent contractor," the employer could not control the manner of performance of the services of an independent contractor, and the employer was not responsible for the personal conduct of independent contractors. In many real estate businesses, salespersons are not considered by the broker to be employees within the common-law definition. They are considered to be independent contractors. It is the purpose of this section to extend the definition of "employee" to those having the common-law status of independent contractors. The effect of this extension is to bring salespersons and associate brokers within the statutory definition of "employee" for purposes of the licensing law. All common-law employees would also be considered to be employees. Since a broker is responsible to the Real Estate Commission for his employees, employees would include, by statutory definition, all salespersons and associate brokers, whether or not they were considered by the broker to be independent contractors.

Note that the definition of "employee" specifically excludes builder-owner salespersons.

> "Limited broker." Any person, partnership, association or corporation engaging in or carrying on the business or act in the capacity of a broker within the Commonwealth exclusively within the limited field or branch of business which applies to cemetery lots, plots and mausoleum spaces or openings.

The licensing law differentiates between brokers generally engaged in the real estate profession and those whose activities are limited to the sale of cemetery lots, plots, and mausoleum spaces and openings. Those persons whose real estate activities are exclusive to this branch may be licensed in this limited field. A limited broker cannot engage in those activities listed in the definition of "broker" without having first qualified for a broker's license. However, a broker may engage in the sales for cemetery lots without having to obtain a limited broker's license.

> "Limited Salesperson." Any person employed by a broker or limited broker to perform duties as defined hereinunder limited broker. No person employed by a broker to perform duties other than those activities as defined hereinunder limited broker shall be required to be licensed as a limited salesperson.

The limited salesperson is also licensed in the limited area of sales of cemetery lots, plots, and mausoleum spaces and openings. The limited salesperson must be in the employ of a limited broker or a broker and cannot engage in the business of sales of cemetery lots and plots even if he is in the employ of the owner of the cemetery or mausoleum.

> "Person." Any individual, corporation, partnership, association or other entity foreign or domestic.

For purposes of the statutory law, persons when referred to includes business entities as well as individuals.

> "Real estate." Any interest or estate in land, whether corporeal, incorporeal, freehold or nonfreehold, whether the land is situated in this Commonwealth or elsewhere including leasehold interests.

The definition in the statute for "real estate" is very broad. It includes *all* interests in real property, including ownership interests and possessory interests. Presumably, the definition is broad enough to encompass security interests, such as mortgages and secured transactions under the Uniform Commercial Code. However, the term real estate is limited to interests and estates in *land.* It is uncertain whether references in the licensing law to real estate would include air rights and mineral rights. Note also that the term "real estate," for purposes of the law, includes land outside the commonwealth.

> "Rental listing referral agent." Any person who owns or manages a business which collects rental information for the purpose of referring prospective tenants to rental units or locations of such units. The term "rental listing referral agent" shall not include any employee or official of any public housing authority created pursuant to State or Federal law.

This section specifically refers to apartment locating services which collate lists of apartments and rental units. The agent, for a fee, provides this list to prospective tenants who then themselves contact the owners or managers of the rental units. Note that it is the *owner* or *manager* of the referral business who is the rental listing referral agent, not the employees who may actually perform the service.

The definition of rental listing referral agent specifically excludes employees and officials of public housing authorities which are created pursuant to federal or state law. The exclusion would only apply to employees and officials of such public housing authorities when acting within the scope of their employment or when acting in an official capacity.

"Salesperson." Any person employed by a licensed real estate broker to list for sale, sell or offer for sale, to buy or offer to buy or to negotiate the purchase or sale or exchange of real estate or to negotiate a loan on real estate or to lease or rent or offer to lease, rent or place for rent any real estate or collect or to offer or attempt to collect rent for the use of real estate for or in behalf of such real estate broker. No person employed by a broker to perform duties other than those activities as defined herein under "broker" shall be required to be licensed as a salesperson.

A "salesperson" is any person employed by a licensed broker to perform the activities included in the definition of "broker." Presumably, the term "salesperson" does not include associate brokers, although they are not specifically excluded from the term "salesperson." In addition, the definition does not include those employed by brokers who do not perform the activities listed in the definition of the term broker. This would include secretarial, maintenance, and accounting personnel in the employ of a broker. Note that under the definition of "salesperson," a person doing *any one* of the activities listed for broker would be considered a salesperson.

"School." Any person, corporation, partnership, association or other entity, foreign or domestic, which conducts classes in real estate subjects, but which is not a college or university duly accredited by the Middle States Association of Colleges and Secondary Schools or equivalent accreditation.

"School" as used in the licensing law means a school which has classes in real estate. This definition of "school" encompasses more than the traditional concept of school. It includes any person or organization which conducts classes in real estate. Therefore, anyone who holds weekend seminars and the like which deal with real estate would be included in the definition.

CHAPTER 3.
APPLICATION OF THE ACT AND PENALTIES

This chapter specifies both criminal and civil sanctions that can result when a person or organization engages in the enumerated broker activities without having properly complied with the requirements of the licensing act. Criminal penalties listed in this chapter are penal in nature. They impose a punishment upon the person or organization that engages in the unlawful activity. In criminal actions, the Commonwealth of Pennsylvania is the prosecuting party even though a private individual may have been harmed by the illegal conduct. The penalties usually associated with criminal actions include monetary fines and imprisonment.

In the civil actions, it is the wronged individual or organization that has the "cause of action" or the right to sue the person or organization that caused the wrong. In such suits, the remedy most commonly sought is monetary damages. However, by statute, claims which normally would result in a valid "cause of action" in a civil action may be barred because of noncompliance with a requirement. Thus, if an individual or an organization engages in any activity that requires a license without having acquired the license, that person or organization may be barred by statute from asserting a claim for damages in court. In such cases, the defendent has a valid defense to the plaintiff's claim because the statute forbids the plaintiff from recovering damages upon the claim.

In addition to specifying criminal penalties and limiting civil action, Chapter 3 includes exemption from the applicability of the licensing act.

> **Section 301. Unlawful to conduct business without license.** From and after the effective date of this act, it shall be unlawful for any person, directly or indirectly, to engage in or conduct, or to advertise or hold himself out as engaging in or conducting the business, or acting in the capacity of a broker or salesperson, limited broker, limited salesperson, builder-owner salesperson, or rental listing referral agent within this Commonwealth without first being licensed as such as provided in this act, unless he is exempted from obtaining a license under the provisions of Section 304.

Section 301 specifies that it is unlawful for any person to engage in any activity which requires a license under the licensing act. Note that the coverage of the law is very broad. Exhibit 4 summarizes this section.

Exhibit 4
SUMMARY OF SECTION 301

Without having been licensed, it is unlawful for any person to
- Engage in
- Conduct or
- Advertise or
- Hold himself out

As a
- Broker,
- Salesperson,
- Limited broker,
- Limited salesperson,
- Builder-owner salesperson, or
- Rental listing referral agent

Unless he is exempt by law.

Section 302. Civil suits. No action or suit shall be instituted, nor recovery be had, in any court of this Commonwealth by any person for compensation for any act done or service rendered, the doing or rendering which is prohibited under the provisions of this act by a person other than a licensed broker, salesperson, limited broker, limited salesperson, builder-owner salesperson or rental listing referral agent, unless such person was duly licensed and registered hereunder as broker or salesperson at the time of offering to perform any such act or service or procuring any promise or contract for the payment of compensation for any such contemplated act or service.

This section bars an individual or organization from suing for fees or commissions for any act which is done or service which is rendered in violation of Section 301. No such civil suit can be maintained unless the person or organization was properly licensed and registered as a broker or salesperson *at the time* of offering to perform any of the enumerated acts or at the time of contracting for the payment.

For example, *X* obtains a listing from *Y* for the sale of *Y*'s property, but at the time of the contract *X* is not duly licensed as a broker under the licensing act. *X* then becomes duly licensed and registered as a broker and thereafter assists in the sale of *Y*'s property. *Y* does not pay *X* the agreed-upon commission. *X* brings suit in the local court of common pleas. *X* may not maintain the lawsuit because, under Section 302, he was barred from asserting his "cause of action" against *Y* because at the time of the contract between *X* and *Y*, *X* was not duly licensed and registered as a broker.

Section 303. Criminal penalties. Any person who shall, after the effective date of this act, engage in or carry on the business, or act in the capacity of a broker, salesperson, limited broker, limited salesperson, builder-owner salesperson or rental listing referral agent, within this Commonwealth, without a license, or shall carry on or continue business after the suspension or revocation of any such license issued to him, or shall employ any person as a salesperson or limited salesperson to whom a license has not been issued, or whose license as such shall have been revoked or suspended, shall be guilty of a summary offense and upon conviction thereof for a first offense shall be sentenced to pay a fine not exceeding $500 or suffer imprisonment, not exceeding three months, or both and for a second or subsequent offense shall be guilty of a felony of the third degree and upon conviction thereof, shall be sentenced to pay a fine of not less than $2,000 but not more than $5,000 or to imprisonment for not less than one year but not more than two years, or both.

This section prescribes criminal penalties for those who engage in broker activities without having a license, those who engage in such activities after their licenses have been suspended or revoked, or a broker who employs a salesperson or limited salesperson who has no license or whose license has been revoked or suspended. Upon conviction of having engaged in any of the proscribed activities, a person is subject to penalties specified in the Act. The first such offense is classified as a "summary offense." Summary offenses are misdemeanors, and such cases are processed through the District Magistrate Court System of Pennsylvania (Justice of the Peace Courts). Upon conviction, the penalty for the first offense is a fine of not more than $500, imprisonment in the county prison for up to three months, or both fine and imprisonment. Upon conviction of the second offense, the crime is a third-degree felony triable in the Court of Common Pleas, and the penalty specified is a fine of between $2,000 and $5,000, imprisonment of not less than one year nor more than two years, or both fine and imprisonment.

Exhibit 5 summarizes the provisions of Section 303.

Exhibit 5
SUMMARY OF SECTION 303

Any person who shall
- Engage in the business,
- Carry on the business,
- Act in the capacity of a
  Broker,
  Salesperson,
  Limited broker,
  Limited salesperson,
  Builder-owner salesperson, or
  Rental listing referral agent
- Without a license, or
- After suspension or revocation of a license, or
- Employ any unlicensed person

Shall be guilty of
- A summary offense and be subject to a fine not exceeding $500, or
- Imprisonment not exceeding three months, or
- Both, and

Upon being found guilty of a subsequent offense shall be subject to
- A fine of at least $2,000 and no more than $5,000, or
- Imprisonment for not less than one nor more than two years, or
- Both.

Section 304. Exclusions. The provisions of this act shall not apply to an owner of real estate with respect to property owned or leased by such owner, provided that in the case of a partnership or corporation, this exclusion shall not extend to more than five of its partners or officers, respectively, but to no other partnership or corporation personnel or employee, except the employees of a public utility acting in the ordinary course of utility-related business under the provisions of Title 66 of the Pennsylvania Consolidated Statutes (relating to public utilities), with respect to negotiating the purchase, sale or lease of property nor shall this act be construed to include in any way the services rendered by an attorney in fact under a duly executed and recorded power of attorney from the owner or lessor (provided such power of attorney is not utilized to circumvent the intent of this act); nor by an attorney at law, nor shall it be held to include a person acting as receiver, trustee in bankruptcy, administrator, executor, trustee, guardian, or while acting under a court order or under the authority of a will or of a trust instrument, nor shall this act apply to the duly elected officer of any banking institution or trust company operating under federal or state banking laws where real estate of the banking institution or trust company only is involved, nor shall they be held to include any officer or employee of a cemetery company who, as incidental to his principal duties and without renumeration therefore, shows lots in such company's cemetery to persons for their use as a family burial lot, and who accepts deposits on such lots for the representatives of the cemetery company, legally authorized to sell the same, nor shall it be held to include any properly licensed auctioneer, under statutes of this State, while performing authorized duties at any bona fide auction.

This section lists exemptions from application of the licensing law. If a person comes within the classes listed in this section, he may engage in the enumerated activities of a broker without having first been duly licensed and registered as either a broker or salesperson. For each class of exemption, the person is exempt *because* of his status as an attorney-at-law; as an employee of a public utility acting in the ordinary course of the utility's business; as a bank officer; as an attorney-in-fact (power of attorney); as an individual acting in a special legal capacity under a court order, as a trustee, or pursuant to a will; or as a licensed auctioneer in a bona fide auction. These exemptions arise because of a special status that an individual enjoys in dealing with real property of another.

Employees of public utilities are specifically exempt provided that they are engaged in negotiating the purchase, sale, or lease of property in the ordinary course of the utility's business. Included in the classification of public utilities would be gas transmission and distribution companies, telephone, telegraph and electric companies, and steam, heat, or water companies. For example, *E*, an employee of the electric power company, offered to purchase from *O*, the owner of real property, an easement for the installation, operation, and maintenance of a power substation. Provided that *E* is offering to purchase on behalf of his employer the public utility, then the activity is exempt and no license would be required of *E*.

The owner of property dealing in property owned or leased by that person is also exempt. Therefore, an individual may sell, lease, and exchange his own property to another without having to be a licensed broker or salesperson. In cases when a corporation or partnership is owner of property, no more than five officers of the corporation or partners of the partnership may sell, lease, or exchange the property without having to be licensed and registered.

The exemption to corporate and partnership property extends only to the officers and partners. Other employees of the corporation or partnership are *not* exempt and each such employee would have to be a broker to sell, lease, or exchange corporate or partnership property. There is a specific exemption in the law for employees of cemetery companies, who as an incident to their regular duties may show cemetery lots and receive deposits from purchasers. This exemption applies only if these employees do not receive separate remuneration from the cemetery company for any lots sold. Such employees could not receive a commission for any sales made.

A person is exempt if he is acting under a power of attorney from the owner authorizing the attorney-in-fact to sell, lease, or exchange property or engage in any of the enumerated activities reserved to brokers. The power of attorney granting the authority to the attorney-in-fact must be *duly executed and recorded* in the Recorder of Deeds Office. The power of attorney must be recorded *before* the attorney-in-fact engages in any of the activities normally reserved to brokers. The exemption for attorneys-in-fact is limited to those situations where the power of attorney is not used to circumvent the intent of the licensing law.

A power of attorney is not necessary in all cases, only when the attorney-in-fact would come within the definition of broker under Section 201. For example, *X*'s father, *F*, as a favor to *X*, places an advertisement in the local newspaper offering to buy a house for *X*. *F* is not authorized under a duly executed and recorded power of attorney to act as *X*'s attorney-in-fact. *F* would not be in violation of the licensure law because, even though he did engage in the enumerated broker activities, it was not for *a fee or other valuable consideration* but merely as a favor to *X*.

Also exempt are properly licensed auctioneers while performing authorized duties at any bona fide auction. A licensed auctioneer may advertise an auction of real property, and may conduct the auction of real property at a bona fide auction. If the auctioneer merely contacts people about purchasing property, negotiates the purchase and sale of property, or performs any activity specifically requiring a license outside the framework of an auction, then the auctioneer would not be exempt. For example, *A*, the auctioneer, has been engaged by the owner to auction property including land. Incident to the auction, *A* places advertisements in the newspapers and posts notices of the sale. *A* answers questions of potential purchasers and conducts the sale of the property at the advertised auction. *A* would be exempt. The advertising is incident to an authorized auction. Note that the action must be "bona fide." An auction with a limited number of bidders and without notice to the general public and an opportunity for others to bid might not qualify as a bona fide auction exempting the auctioneer from licensure.

Exhibit 6 summarizes the exemptions under Section 304.

Exhibit 6
SUMMARY OF SECTION 304

The provisions of the licensing law do not apply to

- An owner dealing in his own property,
- An attorney-in-fact, provided that the power of attorney
  Is from the owner of the property and
  Is duly executed and
  Is recorded and
  Is not used to circumvent the licensing law,
- An attorney-at-law rendering services,
- A receiver,
- A trustee in bankruptcy,
- An administrator,
- An executor,
- A trustee,
- A guardian,
- A person acting under an order of court,
- A person acting under authority of a will or trust instrument,
- A duly elected officer of any bank operating under federal or state banking law,
- An officer or employee of a cemetery company who shows plots as part of regular employment,
- A licensed auctioneer performing authorized services at any bona fide auction, and
- Employees of a public utility acting in an ordinary course of the business of the utility.

CHAPTER 4.
POWERS AND DUTIES OF THE STATE REAL ESTATE COMMISSION – GENERAL

Section 401. Duty to issue licenses. It shall be the duty of the department to issue licenses to individuals, copartnerships and corporations, who shall comply with the provisions of this act.

This section of the law imposes the duty to issue licenses to the Department of State acting through the Commissioner of Professional and Occupational Affairs. Notice that the duty to issue is mandatory provided that the individuals, partnerships, and corporations comply with applicable law and regulation.

Section 402. Approval of schools. Any school which shall offer or conduct any course or courses of study in real estate shall first obtain approval from, and thereafter abide by the rules and regulations of the commission covering such schools.

This section requires schools to seek the prior approval of the Real Estate Commission before conducting any courses in real estate. Remember that the definition of "school" (Section 201) includes anyone who offers classes in real estate.

Section 403. Authority to examine applicants. The commission is empowered to prescribe the subjects to be tested. The department shall arrange for the services of professional testing services to write and administer examinations on behalf of the commission in accordance with commission guidance and approval.

This section grants to the commission the authority to examine applicants for real estate licensure and provides that the department may contract with a testing service to provide for the preparation and the administration of written examinations.

Section 404. Power to promulgate regulations.

(a) The commission shall have the power to promulgate rules or regulations in order to administer and effectuate the purposes of this act. All existing rules or regulations adopted pursuant to the act of May 1, 1929 (P.L.1216, No. 427), known as the "Real Estate Brokers License Act of one thousand nine hundred and twenty-nine," shall remain in full force and effect until modified by the commission. The proposed rules and regulations shall be submitted to the Secretary of the Senate and the Chief Clerk of the House of Representatives who shall cause the rules or regulations to be printed and distributed among all members of both chambers in the same manner as a reorganization plan. If both bodies fail to act within 60 days of receipt of such rules or regulations, or within ten legislative days after receipt, whichever shall last occur, rules or regulations adopted by the commission shall be promulgated pursuant to the provisions of the act of July 31, 1968 (P.L.769, No.240), referred to as the

Commonwealth Documents Law and 45 Pa.C.S. Part II (relating to publication and effectiveness of Commonwealth documents.)

(b) If either chamber disapproves any rule or regulation, such information shall be certified by the Speaker of the House of Representatives or President pro tempore of the Senate to the commission, any such rule or regulation shall not be promulgated as a final rule or regulation.

This section gives the Real Estate Commission the power to promulgate rules and regulations in order to administer and carry out the purposes of the Real Estate Licensing Act of 1980. Until such regulations are effective, the law provides that the regulations promulgated under the prior law, the Real Estate Brokers Licensing Act of 1929 shall continue in effect. The law also provides a mechanism for adoption of regulations which bypasses the time consuming procedures required for the adoption under the Administrative Agency Law. At the time such regulations are adopted, the former regulations adopted under the 1929 Act will be repealed.

Since law passed by the legislature and signed by the governor take precedence over administrative regulations, any inconsistency between the 1980 Act and the new regulations issued pursuant to the 1929 Act would be resolved in favor of the provisions of the new law.

Section 405. Duty to keep records confidential. Neither the Commissioner of Profession and Occupational Affairs, any member of the commission, nor any deputy, secretary, representative, clerk or other employee of the Commonwealth, shall directly or indirectly, willfully, exhibit, publish, divulge, or make known to any person or persons any record, report, statement, letter, or any other matter, fact or thing except in accordance with the laws of this Commonwealth dealing with the public's right to access to Commonwealth proceedings and records. A person violating the provisions of this section shall be guilty of a misdemeanor and sentenced to pay a fine not exceeding $1,000: Provided, however, that the provisions of this section shall not apply to any ruling or decision of the commission, with the record relative thereto, and upon which the same was founded, which ruling or decision shall have been duly made and entered under and in accordance with the provisions of this act, after investigation and hearing as hereinafter provided. All such records shall, immediately upon the entry of such ruling or decision, become public records of the department, subject to inspection by any person interested.

This section imposes a duty on the Real Estate Commission to retain the confidentiality of records. No one may, either directly or indirectly, willfully publish, divulge, or make known to any person records or facts except in accordance with existing law.

The section imposes a penalty of a $1,000 fine for a violation of the restrictions.

The section specifically exempts rulings and decisions of the commission which are incident to a regular proceeding against a license after investigation and hearing. The records, evidence, and transcript of testimony are public record and disclosure of any such records or evidence would not be a violation of this section of the law.

Section 406. Administration and enforcement. The commission shall have the power and its duty shall be to administer and enforce the laws of the commonwealth relating to those activities involving real estate for which licensing is required under this act and to instruct and require its agents to bring prosecutions for unauthorized and unlawful practice.

This section grants to the Real Estate Commission the authority to enforce the provisions of the licensing law and imposes a mandatory duty on the commission to instruct and require its agents to enforce the law and regulations.

CHAPTER 5.
QUALIFICATIONS AND APPLICATIONS FOR LICENSES

SUBCHAPTER A. GENERAL

Section 501. Reputation; inactive licensee.

(a) Licenses shall be granted only to persons who bear a good reputation for honesty, trustworthiness, integrity and competence to transact the business broker, salesperson, limited broker, limited salesperson, builder-owner salesperson or rental listing referral agent, in such manner as to safeguard the interest of the public, and only after satisfactory proof of such qualifications has been presented to the commission as it shall be regulation require.

(b) Any person who remains inactive for a period of five years without renewing his licenses shall, prior to having a license reissued to him, submit to and pass an examination.

This section prescribes the reputation requirements of applicants for licensure. The actual mechanics of proof of honesty, trustworthiness, integrity, and competence are left for the commission to provide for by regulation.

A license is not good forever; it has to be renewed. The law requires that a licensee who has not renewed his license for five consecutive years must retake an examination. The law does not specify that the examination be the same as is required of licensees being licensed for the first time. Note that there is no requirement for an additional apprenticeship. Presumably, the licensee has fulfilled the requirements or a license would not have been issued.

In addition to the requirement of reputation, the law provides a list of qualifications for licensure as a broker.

SUBCHAPTER B. BROKER'S LICENSE

Section 511. Qualifications for license. The applicant for a broker's license, shall as a condition precedent to obtaining a license, take the broker's license examination and score a passing grade. Prior to taking the examination:

(1) The applicant shall be at least 21 years of age.

(2) The applicant shall be a high school graduate or shall produce proof satisfactory to the commission of an education equivalent thereto.

(3) The applicant shall have completed 16 semester credit hours of 15 hours each in real estate instruction in areas of study prescribed by the rules of the commission.

(4) The applicant shall have been engaged full time as a salesperson for at least three years or possess educational or experience qualifications which the commission deems to be the equivalent thereof.

The applicant for a broker's license must pass a written examination and meet the other qualifications listed. The qualifications must be met *before* the applicant is able to sit for the examination. Note that there is an age requirement of 21 years, a general educational requirement of a high school diploma or its equivalent, and a specific educational and experience background requirement.

Note also that the real estate educational requirement can be satisfied only in areas of study approved by the commission. The law requires that the applicant for a broker's license have at least three years' experience as a *full-time* salesperson. Mere licensure for three years as a salesperson is not enough. However, under certain circumstances, the commission has the authority to grant an applicant a waiver of the three years' experience requirement.

Exhibit 7 summarizes the qualifications for broker's license.

Exhibit 7
QUALIFICATIONS FOR A BROKER'S LICENSE

The applicant for broker's license must

- Be at least 21 years of age,
- Be a high school graduate (or its equivalent),
- Have completed 16 semester credit hours on real estate instruction, and
- Have engaged full time as a salesperson for three years (or equivalent).

Section 512. Application for license.

(a) An application for license as real estate broker shall be made in writing, to the department, upon a form provided for the purpose by the department and shall contain such information as to the applicant as the commission shall require.

(b) The application shall be accompanied by two photographs of the applicant or in the case of a copartnership, association or corporation of the applicant members or officers thereof.

(c) The application shall state the place of business for which such license is desired.

(d) The application shall be received by the commission within three years of the date upon which the applicant took the examination.

After an individual of good reputation (Section 501) meets the qualifications for licensure and passes the written examination (Section 511), he does not automatically receive a broker's license. The applicant must submit an application to the commission on the form provided. In addition to information required by the commission, the applicant must state the address of his place of business and include two photographs of himself. The application must be received no later than three years after the applicant has taken the written examination for brokers.

Section 513. Corporations, partnerships and associations. If the applicant for a broker's license is a corporation, partnership or association, then the provisions of Sections 511 and 512 shall apply to the individual designated as broker of record. The employees of said corporation, partnership or association actually engaging in or intending to engage in the real estate business shall meet the provisions of Sections 521 and 522.

Since the real estate business may be conducted by an association of individuals either as partners or as a corporation, licensure of the corporation must include licensure of the persons who will actually be engaged in real estate brokerage. Remember that there is only one individual in either a partnership or corporation who is designated as being responsible to the commission for the operation of the business. This broker of record must comply with the requirements of the preceding two sections (Sections 511 and 512) and all partners of the partnership and all officers and employees of the corporation who will actually be engaged or *intend to be engaged* in the enumerated activities of real estate broker must meet the requirements of salespersons (Sections 521 and 522).

SUBCHAPTER C. SALESPERSON'S LICENSE

Section 521. Qualifications for license. Each applicant shall as a condition precedent to obtaining a license, take the salesperson license examination and score a passing grade. Prior to taking the examination:

(1) The applicant shall be at least 18 years of age.

(2) The applicant shall have completed four semester credit hours of 15 hours each in real estate instruction in areas of study prescribed by the rules of the commission.

This section lists the qualifications for salesperson's licenses. Note that the application must meet the qualifications for salespersons *prior to* taking the examination. The age qualification is 18 years, and there is no general educational requirement for a high school diploma or its equivalent as there is with brokers. Presumably, a licensed salesperson can complete high school during his three-year experience requirement before sitting for the broker's examination. There is a specific educational requirement for courses in real estate, and as with the broker's requirement the areas of study must be approved by the commission. Note that reputation prerequisites specified in Section 501 applies to salesperson applicants. Exhibit 8 summarizes the qualifications for salespersons.

Exhibit 8
QUALIFICATIONS FOR A SALESPERSON

The applicant for salesperson's license must

- Be at least 18 years of age,
- Have completed four semester credit hours in real estate instruction, and
- Meet the prerequisites for honesty, integrity, trustworthiness, and competency.

Section 522. Application for license.

(a) An application for a license as salesperson shall be made, in writing to the department, upon a form provided for the purpose by the department, and shall contain such information as to the applicant, as the commission shall require.

(b) The applicant shall submit a sworn statement by the broker with whom he desires to be affiliated certifying that the broker will actively supervise and train the applicant.

(c) The application shall be received by the commission within three years of the date upon which the applicant took the examination.

The application requires that the salesperson applicant submit a sworn statement from the broker for whom the salesperson will work certifying the broker's willingness to supervise and train the applicant salesperson. Note that the supervision and training must be "active." The application must be received by the commission within three years of the date when the salesperson applicant took the written examination.

SUBCHAPTER D. LIMITED BROKER'S LICENSE

Section 531. Qualifications for license. Each applicant for a limited broker's license shall as a condition to obtaining a license take the limited broker's license examination and score a passing grade. Prior to taking the examination:

(1) The applicant shall be at least 21 years of age.
(2) The applicant shall have been engaged full time as a salesperson or limited salesperson for at least three years or possess educational or experience qualifications which the commission deems to be the equivalent thereof.

A limited broker is a person or business organization engaged in the sale of cemetery lots and plots or mausoleum spaces or openings. The limited broker's practice is restricted to the sale of this specialized interest in real estate. The limited salesperson does not have authority to engage in any other activities of real estate broker. However, the reverse is not true: A licensed broker can engage in the sale of cemetery lots, plots, and mausoleum spaces and openings without having to be a limited broker as well. Remember also that a full-time employee of a cemetery company, who as an incident to his regular duties as a full-time employee of the company shows cemetery lots and collects deposits, does not have to be licensed as a limited broker or limited salesperson, provided that no extra remuneration is paid the employee for such activities (Section 304).

Prior to taking the special examination for limited brokers, the applicant shall be at least 21 years of age and shall have been engaged *full-time* as a salesperson or limited salesperson or possess equivalent experience. Note that the applicant's three-year apprenticeship need not be in the limited field but can be in the general real estate field. There is, however, a general educational requirement of a high school diploma.

Section 532. Application for license.

(a) An application for a license as a limited broker shall be made, in writing, to the department, upon a form provided for the purpose by the department and shall contain such information as to the applicant, as the commission shall require.

(b) The applicant shall have completed four semester credit hours of 15 hours each in real estate instruction in areas of study prescribed by the rules of the commission.

(c) The application shall be received by the commission within three years of the date upon which the applicant took the examination.

This section specifies the application process for limited brokers. It gives the commission the authority to prescribe the application form. The application is to be received within three years of the date when the limited broker applicant took the written examination. Note that this section includes an educational requirement in the real estate area.

Section 533. Corporations, partnerships, associations or other entities. If the applicant for a limited brokers license is a corporation, partnership, association, or other entity, foreign or domestic, then the provisions of Sections 531 and 532 shall apply to the individual designated as Broker of Record, as well as those members actually engaging in or intending to engage in the real estate business.

Corporate and partnership businesses engaged in the sale of cemetery lots and mausoleum spaces and openings shall designate a broker of record who is responsible to the commission for complying with all rules and regulations. All partners and officers and employees of the corporation who engage in the sale of lots and spaces or who intend to do so must also be licensed.

SUBCHAPTER E. LIMITED SALESPERSON'S LICENSE

Section 541. Qualifications for license. The applicant for a limited salesperson's license shall be at least 18 years of age.

The only qualifications for limited licensure are that the applicant be 18 years of age and that the applicant meet the reputation requirements of Section 501.

Section 542. Application for license.

(a) An application for a license as a limited salesperson shall be made, in writing, to the department, upon a form provided for the purpose by the department, and shall contain such information as to the applicant, as the commission shall require.

(b) The applicant for a license shall submit a sworn affidavit by the broker or limited broker with whom he desires to be affiliated certifying that the broker will actively supervise and train the applicant and certifying the truth and accuracy of the certification of the applicant.

This section specifies the application procedure for limited salespersons. The applicant must submit a sworn affidavit from the broker or limited broker for whom he intends to work. The broker or limited broker must certify that the broker or limited broker will actively supervise and train the limited salesperson and must also certify to the truth and accuracy of the application. There is no general or specific educational prerequisite for limited salesperson.

SUBCHAPTER F. BUILDER-OWNER SALESPERSON'S LICENSE

Section 551. Qualifications for license. Each applicant for a builder-owner salesperson's license, shall as a condition precedent to obtaining a license, take the standard real estate salesperson's license examination and score a passing grade. Prior to taking the examination:

(1) The applicant shall be 18 years of age.

(2) The applicant shall be employed by a builder-owner possessing those qualifications as contained in Section 501.

As defined in the licensing law, a "builder-owner salesperson" is any person who is in the full-time employ of a builder-owner of single- and multifamily dwellings within the commonwealth. The builder-owner salesperson is authorized and empowered to sell, lease, or exchange real estate owned by the builder-owner.

The applicant for builder-owner salesperson must pass the written examination for salesperson after having met all of the qualifications listed in the law. The applicant must be 18 years of age. The applicant must work for a builder-owner who meets the qualifications as to reputation for honesty, trustworthiness, integrity, and competence to transact the real estate brokerage business. However, the law does not specify by which method the builder-owner's reputation is to be verified. There is no general or specific educational prerequisite listed for builder-owner salesperson.

Section 552. Application for license.

(a) An application for a license as a builder-owner salesperson shall be made, in writing to the department, upon a form provided for the purpose by the department, and shall contain such information as to the applicant as the commission shall require.

(b) The applicant shall submit a sworn statement by the builder-owner by whom he is employed certifying to such employment.

(c) The application shall be received by the commission within three years of the date upon which the applicant took the examination.

This section specifies the application process for builder-owner salespersons. The application must be made on a form prepared by the commission. The applicant must provide a certificate from the builder-owner certifying that the applicant is employed by the builder-owner. The builder-owner salesperson must apply within three years of taking the examination.

SUBCHAPTER G. RENTAL LISTING REFERRAL AGENT'S LICENSE

Section 561. Qualifications for license. The qualification for licensure as a rental listing referral agent shall be the same as those set forth in Sections 521 and 522 except that the applicant need not be affiliated with a broker.

The qualifications for rental listing referral agent are the same as those of salesperson, and the application process is the same except that the rental listing referral agent is not required to be in the employ of a licensed broker. Remember that under the definition of "rental listing referral agent" (Section 201), the activities include the referral of prospective tenants to the owners of dwelling units. The rental listing referral agent would have to be licensed as a salesperson and be in the employ of a broker before engaging in the activities associated with real estate brokerage. The rental listing referral agent is responsible to the commission for compliance with all rules and regulations of the commission.

CHAPTER 6.
DUTIES OF LICENSEES

Section 601. Duty of brokers and limited brokers to maintain office.

(a) Each resident licensed broker (which term in this section shall include limited broker) shall maintain a fixed office within this commonwealth. The original license of a broker and of each licensee *employed by such* broker shall be *prominently displayed in an office of the broker.* The address of the office shall be designated on the current renewal form. In case of removal of a broker's office from the designated location, all licensees registered at that location shall make application to the commission before such removal or within ten days thereafter, designating the new location of the office, and shall pay the required fees, whereupon the commission shall issue a renewal form at the new location for the unexpired period, if the new location complies with the terms of this act. Each licensed broker shall maintain a sign on the outside of his office indicating the proper licensee brokerage name.

(b) If the applicant for a broker's license intends to maintain more than one place of business within the commonwealth, he shall apply for and obtain an additional license in his name at each branch office. Every such application shall state the location of such branch office. Effective 24 months after the effective date of this act, each branch office shall be under the direction and supervision of a manager who is either the broker of record or an associate broker: provided, however, that such broker of record or an associate broker may direct and supervise more than one branch office.

Section 601 imposes the duty on all brokers and limited brokers to maintain places of business at fixed locations within the commonwealth. The licenses of the broker of record and the licenses of all salespersons and limited salespersons must be prominently displayed in an office of the broker. If a broker of record changes locations, all licensees must change their record address. The commission must be notified either before the location is changed or within ten days of any change. This section also requires the licensed broker to maintain a sign outside his office indicating the proper licensed brokerage name.

Section 601(b) requires that a broker who wishes to maintain more than one location must apply for and obtain a license for each location. This license is issued in the name of the broker of record. Every office must have the broker of record or an associate broker employed by the broker of record in charge. The broker of record or the associate broker can supervise more than one branch office. The effect of this is to permit an associate broker to be in charge of a branch office, but the broker of record is still responsible to the commission for the operation of the branch office and the conduct of the associate broker and the salespersons at the branch office.

The law does not place any limit on the number of branch offices that may be maintained by a broker so long as the broker and associate brokers under his control can properly supervise the branch offices.

Section 602. Nonresident licensees.

(a) A nonresident of this Commonwealth may be licensed as a broker or a salesperson, upon complying with all provisions and conditions as promulgated by the commission.

(b) In connection with the application of a nonresident of this Commonwealth for a license as broker or salesperson, the commission may accept, in lieu of the recommendations and statements otherwise required to accompany the application for such licensure, the license as broker or salesperson issued to such applicant by the proper authority of the state of his licensure. In such cases the licensee need not maintain a place of business within this Commonwealth. It is hereby expressly stipulated, that the provisions of this subsection shall apply to licensed brokers and salespersons of those states under the laws of which similar recognition and courtesies are extended to licensed brokers and salespersons of this Commonwealth.

Nonresidents of the commonwealth are permitted to be licensed by the commission under special procedures. A nonresident of Pennsylvania may be licensed without having to maintain an office at a fixed location within the commonwealth and without having to successfully pass the Pennsylvania brokers, salesperson, or limited broker's examination and other qualifications (Sections 511, 521, 531). The general requirement is that the person be licensed and in good standing as a broker, salesperson, or limited broker in his home state, and that his home state accord similar nonresident status to Pennsylvania brokers, salesperson, and limited broker licensees. The special status accorded by each licensing state to the licensees of the other state is sometimes referred to as "reciprocity." The exact procedure for implementing the reciprocal licensing is left to regulation by the commission.

Remember that this nonresident status of brokers, salespersons, and limited brokers only deals with the necessity of maintaining a business location in Pennsylvania and with special procedures for licensing. An applicant for broker, salesperson, or limited broker is not required to be a resident of Pennsylvania as a qualification for licensure. Nonresidents can be licensed as brokers, salespersons, and limited brokers without reciprocity. However, in cases where there is no reciprocity, nonresident brokers and limited brokers must maintain a business location within the Commonwealth and brokers, salespersons, and limited brokers must meet Pennsylvania qualifications and pass the Pennsylvania licensure examination.

Section 603. Employment of associate brokers, salesperson. No associate broker or salesperson (which term in this section shall include limited salesperson) shall be employed by any other broker than is designated upon the renewal form issued to said associate broker or said salesperson. Whenever a licensed salesperson or associate broker desires to change his employment from one licensed broker to another, he shall notify the commission in writing at least ten days prior to the intended date of change, pay the required fee, and return his current renewal license. The commission, shall, upon receipt of acknowledgement from the new broker, of the change of employment forthwith issue a new renewal form and pocket card, but in the interim at such time as the change in affiliation of the salesperson or associate broker occurs, he shall maintain a copy of the notification sent to the commissioner as his temporary license pending receipt of his renewal form. It shall be the duty of the applicant to notify the commission if a new renewal form or other pertinent communication is not received from the commission within 30 days.

This section prohibits salespersons, limited salespersons, and associate brokers from being employed by anyone other than the broker named upon their renewal form. The section also outlines the procedure that an associate broker, salesperson, or limited salesperson must use in order to change employing brokers. Presumably, this same procedure would be applicable to a broker of record who terminates his practice and becomes an associate broker. The moving licensee must notify the commission in writing of the intended move at least ten days in advance. The letter of notification should include the licensee's current renewal license and the required fee. The new employing broker must verify the employment with the commission and, upon such acknowledgment from the new employing broker, the commission shall issue a new renewal and pocket card. In the interim between the termination of employment with the former broker and the receipt of the new renewal form and pocket card listing the new employing broker, a copy of the notification to the commission shall temporarily serve as the license until receipt of the new renewal form and pocket card. If the new renewal form and pocket card are not received within thirty days, the licensee is charged with the duty of notifying the commission.

Section 604 is the largest section in the Real Estate Licensing Act. It contains more substantive law than any of the other sections and is a major source of examination questions, and the examinee may be overwhelmed by its 22 subparagraphs.

To provide a framework for understanding and organizing the material, the section may be divided into two general classifications. First, the section includes those substantive rules which impose mandatory duties on persons coming within the scope of the Real Estate Licensing Act. Second, the section includes substantive rules which prohibit those persons subject to the law from engaging in certain acts. Some of the mandatory duties and prohibited acts apply to all licensees, including brokers, salespersons, associate brokers, rental listing referral agents, builder-owner salespersons, limited brokers, and limited salespersons. Other mandatory duties or prohibited acts apply only to brokers and limited brokers and to salespersons, limited salespersons, and associate brokers.

After you have read through the section, you will find Exhibits 14 and 15 on pages 55 and 56 helpful summarizing the material. (In each, the number in brackets indicates the subparagraph reference.)

Section 604. Prohibited acts. The commission may upon its own motion, and shall promptly upon the verified complaint in writing of any person setting forth a complaint under this section, ascertain the facts and, if warranted, hold a hearing for the suspension or revocation of a license or for the imposition of fines not exceeding $500. The commission shall have power to refuse a license for cause or to suspend or revoke a license or to levy fines up to $500 where the said license has been obtained by false representation, or by fraudulent act or conduct, or where a licensee, in performing or attempting to perform any of the acts mentioned herein, is found guilty of.

This section is one of the most important in the licensing law. It specifies the acts which are prohibited by licensees and grants the power to the Real Estate Commission to investigate complaints either on its own impetus or upon a properly filed complaint by any person. After investigation, the commission can hold hearings of the alleged violation of the prohibited acts and upon conviction punish an offending licensee by suspending or revoking a licensee's license or imposing a monetary fine. The commission also has the right to refuse or revoke a licensee's license if the license was obtained by misrepresentation or fraud.

Exhibit 9 summarizes the powers of the commission. A thorough understanding of each of the prohibited acts is essential to successful completion of the examination as well as proper practice of the real estate brokerage profession.

Exhibit 9
POWERS OF THE COMMISSION TO INVESTIGATE AND PUNISH VIOLATIONS OF THE LICENSING LAW

The commission may
- Upon its own motion, or
- Upon verified complaint in writing

Do the following:
- Ascertain facts, and
- Hold hearings.

If a license was obtained by false representation or fraud, or if a licensee is found guilty of violating the provisions of the law, the commission may
- Suspend a license,
- Revoke a license, or
- Impose a fine not to exceed $500.

Section 604 continued by listing 22 specifically prohibited acts. Each prohibited act is listed and discussed below.

(1) Making any substantial misrepresentation.

A misrepresentation is a statement of fact or a statement of law which is false. In reliance or the misrepresentation, another, who had the reasonable right to rely upon the statement of fact or law, is monetarily damaged. A misrepresentation can be either intentional or negligent. A misrepresentation is intentional when the person making the misrepresentation has actual knowledge that the statement of fact or law is false and intended to defraud the person to whom the statement is made. The misrepresentation is calculated to deceive the other. For example, *X*, a broker, knows that the lot being offered for sale to *Y* is subject to periodic flooding and that the lot would not be approved for residential construction. *Y* asks *X* whether *X* knows of any reason why a house could not be constructed on the lot. *X* replied that there is not. *Y* purchases the lot, and the municipality denies *Y* a building permit because the lot is located in a floodplain. *X* has made an intentional misrepresentation of fact to *Y* upon which *Y* relied to his detriment. Even though as a broker *X* represented the seller of the lot, he still owed a duty to *Y* *not* to make a substantial misrepresentation. Now, suppose that in this example *Y* had asked *X*, "Is this lot in a floodplain?" and without bothering to check the fact, *Y* replies, "It is not in a floodplain." *Y* purchases the lot but later finds that he cannot build a house there. In this case, *X* made a representation of fact without having first checked to see if the lot was in a floodplain. Since, under most circumstances, *Y* would have the right to rely upon the statement of a licensed broker, and since *Y* was damaged, *X* has made a negligent misrepresentation. It would be no defense that the owner of the property did not advise *X* that the lot was located in a floodplain.

Note that the misrepresentation must be *substantial.* Under most circumstances, a substantial misrepresentation would be a misrepresentation that affects the financial interest of the person who has detrimentally relied upon the misrepresentation. For example, if *X*, a licensed broker, were to state to *Y*, the purchaser of a building lot, that the area of the lot was one-fourth acre. *Y* purchases the lot and later discovers that there were 250 square feet less than one-fourth acre. If the lack of acreage had no effect upon its market price, *Y* would have less land but would not have been damaged by the misrepresentation of *X*, and *X* would not be guilty of substantial misrepresentation.

Exhibit 10 summarizes subparagraph (1).

Exhibit 10
SUBSTANTIAL MISREPRESENTATIONS

A substantial misrepresentation is

- A statement of fact,
- Which is known (intentionally) or which should have been known (negligently) to have been false,
- Designed to deceive or defraud another,
- And the other, in reliance on the statement of fact, is monetarily damaged.

(2) Making any false promise of a character likely to influence, persuade or induce any person to enter into any contract or agreement when he could not or did not intend to keep such promise.

The prohibition in this subparagraph makes it unlawful to make a *false* promise which the promissor does not intend to keep. Not only must the promise be false, but the promise itself must be the inducement for a person to enter into a contract. For example, *X*, a broker who is also a real estate developer, was engaged in the sale of recreational lots. He promised *Y*, a lot purchaser, that his lot would be adjacent to a "to-be-constructed lake." In reality, the rock strata under the proposed lake would not hold water and *X* knew this. The false promise induced *Y* into purchasing the "lakefront" property. *X* would be guilty of making a false promise.

(3) Pursuing a continued and flagrant course of misrepresentation or making of false promises through salesperson, associate broker, other persons, or any medium of advertising, or otherwise.

This subparagraph is closely related to the previous two. Under this subparagraph, the broker himself may still be guilty of either false promises or misrepresentation if the salespersons or associate brokers under the broker's supervision and control violate the prohibitions of the above subparagraphs. The broker would also be guilty if any misrepresentation or false promises were made by the broker through any person, any medium of advertising, or otherwise. For example, broker *X* instructs his salesperson *Y* to tell *P*, the purchaser of a building lot that the zoning is commercial when, in fact, the zoning is residential only. In reliance on the statement of *Y*, *P* purchases the lot for the purposes of constructing a gasoline service station and is monetarily damaged by the misrepresentation. *Both* the broker and the salesperson would be guilty of a misrepresentation, even though it was only the salesperson who actually made the misrepresentation. The broker cannot "hide behind" another to escape liability if the other was acting at the instruction of the broker in doing an unlawful act.

(4) Any misleading or untruthful advertising, or using any other trade name or insignia or membership in any real estate association or organization, of which the licensee is not a member.

This subparagraph has two parts. The first part prohibits misleading or untruthful advertising. Notice that there is no requirement that anyone detrimentally rely upon the untruthful or misleading advertising, and there is no requirement in the law that the licensee *intends* that the advertising be untruthful or misleading. For example, a promotional brochure published by broker *X* shows a city bus driving through the advertised subdivision. At the time the picture was taken, the bus had made a wrong turn into the subdivision and in reality there was no public transportation in or near the subdivision. *X* knows that there is no city bus service to the subdivision, and he does not intend to deceive anyone. No one purchased a lot in reliance upon the city bus service being provided to the subdivision. Nevertheless, *X* would be guilty of misleading or untruthful advertising. The advertising in the brochure was both misleading and untruthful.

Note that the prohibited advertising does not have to be misleading *and* untruthful; it need only be misleading *or* untruthful. Thus, truthful advertising which is misleading is also prohibited. For example, in the previous case, if there were city bus service to the subdivision, but the service was provided only during the week of the annual country fair, the advertising brochure would have reflected the truth that city bus service is provided, but might have misled a purchaser into believing that city bus service was provided on a regular basis.

The second part of this subparagraph prohibits the use of a trade name, insignia, or membership in a real estate association to which the licensee does not belong. This is designed to prohibit the use of the word "REALTOR®" by nonmembers of the National Association of Realtors®. The word REALTOR and the insignia ® are registered trademarks of that organization and reserved for use by members only or others only upon prior written permission.

(5) Failure to comply with the following requirements:

(i) all deposits or other moneys accepted by every person, holding a real estate broker license under the provisions of this act, shall be retained by such real estate broker pending consummation or termination of the transaction involved, and shall be accounted for in the full amount thereof at the time of the consummation or termination;

(ii) every salesperson and associate broker promptly on receipt by him of a deposit or other moneys on any transaction in which he is engaged on behalf of his broker-employer, shall pay over the deposit to the broker;

(iii) a broker shall not commingle the money or other property of his principal with his own;

(iv) every broker shall immediately deposit such moneys, of whatever kind or nature, belonging to others, in a separate custodial or trust fund account maintained by the broker with some bank or recognized depository until the transaction involved is consummated or terminated, at which time the broker shall account for the full amount received. Under no circumstances shall a broker permit any advance payment of funds belonging to others to be deposited in the broker's business or personal account, or to be commingled with any funds he may have on deposit; or

(v) every broker shall keep records of all funds deposited therein, which records shall indicate clearly the date and from whom he received money, the date deposited, the dates of withdrawals, and other pertinent information concerning the transaction, and shall show clearly for whose account the money is deposited and to whom the money belongs. All such records and funds shall be subject to inspection by the commission. Such separate custodial or trust fund account shall designate the broker, as trustee, and such account must provide for withdrawal of funds without previous notice. All such records shall be available to the commission, or its representatives, immediately after proper demand or after written notice given, or upon written notice given to the depository.

This paragraph details the responsibilities of the licensee with regard to monies belonging to others received by the licensee incident to a real estate transaction.

Subparagraph (i) establishes the requirement that monies received by a licensee shall be retained by the broker pending the settlement *or* termination of the transaction. The broker must *account* for the full account at the time of termination or consummation of the transaction. Note that the term "account" is used in its technical and legal sense. This is not merely a settlement statement or an enumeration of the receipts and disbursements. The word "account" means that the broker is responsible and is under a fiduciary duty to the parties to the transaction. For example, if the broker were to misplace his checkbook, and another were to fraudulently write a check which depleted the account, the broker must "account" to the parties and make good any loss. The duty to account not only applies when a fraudulent act is involved but when the broker mistakenly makes a disbursement. For example, *X*, a licensed broker, wishes to prorate taxes between the buyer and seller. *X*, who is holding buyer's money pending settlement, believes that the seller has prepaid the taxes and prorates the taxes based upon this belief. Later, it is discovered that the refund of taxes made by the buyer was in error and the buyer was required to pay the entire amount of the tax in order to protect his equity in the property. The broker must *account* to the buyer for the disbursement made to the seller and restore the funds out of his own pocket to the buyer. The broker may seek to recover the misapplied funds from the seller, but the buyer has direct recourse against the broker.

Notice that the broker must account to the parties upon consummation of the transaction or its termination. Therefore, if a transaction were to terminate before its consummation, the duty to account applies on the termination. If the buyer is unable to complete the transaction, the broker must account to the appropriate party for the earnest money deposit.

Subparagraph (ii) requires that each salesperson and associate broker pay over to the designated broker any monies received incident to a transaction. There is no time limit specified for payment to the brokers. The statute calls for "prompt" payment. The circumstances will vary with the facts of each case. For example, if an earnest money deposit is received by *Y*, a licensed salesperson, on Friday evening, "prompt" payment may be made to the broker for deposit on the following Monday morning, more than 48 hours later. However, if earnest money payment is made on Tuesday morning and the money is not turned over to the broker until Thursday morning, the payment may not be considered to be "prompt." Note that there is no authority for a salesperson or associate broker to have his own escrow, custodial, or trust account. It is the broker of record who is responsible to the commission and accountable to the parties for funds entrusted incident to a real estate transaction.

Subparagraph (iii) prohibits a broker from commingling deposited funds with personal or business funds. The prohibition not only includes money but other property as well. However, the circumstances under which property other than money is received on deposit are very rare.

The funds which are received, such as earnest money deposits, are not the property of the broker and must be segregated from his own funds. Even if there is a separate bookkeeping entry on the broker's business account books, this is not considered to be a separate account and, for purposes of the statute, would be considered commingling. The law requires a separate account.

For example, *X*, a licensed broker, received an earnest money deposit from *B*, the buyer of residential property, on behalf of *S*, the broker's client who is seller of the property. The deposit amount is $2,000. The amount is also the amount of the anticipated fee that will be paid from *S* to *X*. The listing contract between *S* and *X* gives *X* the right to receive the fee upon securing a buyer of *S's* property. *X's* right to receive the fee is not contingent upon the consummation of the transaction between *S* and *B*, but is payable upon performance of the service by *X*. Instead of depositing the earnest money in a separate account, *X* deposits it to his business account and uses it to pay salaries. The transaction is consummated, and *B* takes title to the property as provided for in the agreement between *B* and *S*. *X* would be in violation of the law because he does not have the right to immediately receive the deposit made by *B*. His right was to require *S* to pay the fee at the time the services were performed, not to deposit the earnest money from *B* to his business account.

Subparagraph (iv) requires the broker to *immediately* deposit monies received from others incident to a real estate transaction to a custodial or trust account. Note that while a salesperson or associate broker must turn over the money "promptly," the broker must deposit the funds "immediately." However, immediate deposit probably means as immediately as possible under the circumstances of each case. For example, if the broker were to receive an earnest money deposit during the evening hours after the banks have closed, the broker would probably not be required to make a separate night deposit of the funds. The following business day would be in compliance with the requirement of "immediate" deposit. A deposit two business days later would probably not be in compliance unless special circumstances existed which made it impossible for the broker to deposit the funds.

Subparagraph (iv) also requires that the custodial or trust account be maintained in a bank or recognized depository. Presumably, a savings bank or savings and loan would be considered a recognized depository; however, under most circumstances, a broker may not deposit the money in an interest-bearing account without the prior agreement of the parties, and the broker would not be entitled to receive the interest paid on any such account.

This subparagraph also prohibits a broker from making any advanced payments of funds. For example, *X*, a licensed broker, is holding an earnest money deposit in his escrow account. *S*, the seller, has accepted the buyer's offer. *S* must move to another city and requests that the broker pay over to *S* a portion of the earnest money so that he can complete his travel to the other city. *X* advances $500 to *S* from the earnest money deposit. *X* would be in violation because he has advanced payment of funds which do not technically belong to *S* until the delivery by *S* of the deed and compliance by the parties with all contract conditions at settlement.

Subparagraph (v) specifies the records which must be maintained by the broker. Exhibit 11 indicates these records.

Exhibit 11
RECORDS TO BE MAINTAINED BY THE BROKER UNDER SECTION 604(5)(v)

- The date the money was received,
- From whom the money was received,
- The date the money was deposited,
- The date the money was withdrawn,
- Other pertinent information,
- For whose account the money is deposited, and
- To whom the money belongs.

All records must be made available to the commission or its authorized representatives upon proper demand.

Exhibit 12 summarizes the requirement of the custodial, trust, or escrow account.

Exhibit 12
REQUIREMENTS OF THE CUSTODIAL, TRUST, OR ESCROW ACCOUNTS UNDER SECTION 604(5)(v)

The account must be maintained in:
- A bank, or
- Recognized depository,

The account must name the broker as trustee, and
The account must provide for withdrawals without prior notice to the bank or depository.

(6) Failing to preserve for three years following its consummation records relating to any real estate transaction.

This subparagraph places upon the licensee the duty to preserve for three years records relating to any real estate transaction. The law is not very specific as to which records must be maintained. Presumably, all contracts, agreements, and settlement statements must be maintained for only those transactions in which the broker was involved. If a transaction is not "consummated" within the meaning of the law, the records need not be preserved. However, the broker should probably preserve all records whether or not the transaction is consummated. Transactions other than the purchase and sale of property are also included. Therefore, all management or consulting agreements should also be retained for the prescribed period.

(7) Acting for more than one party in a transaction without the knowledge and consent in writing of all parties for whom he acts.

This is a "conflict of interest" prohibition. A conflict of interest arises when the broker's personal interests conflict with those of his client, or when the broker, in his representative capacity, attempts to represent two or more parties whose interests are adverse. Since a fiduciary relationship exists between the client and the broker, the client is entitled to rely upon the advice of the broker. If the broker's interests conflict with the client's, it is difficult for the broker to keep the client's interests foremost. If a broker represents more than one party to a transaction, the broker cannot exercise sound judgment on behalf of both clients because what is favorable to one may not be favorable to the other. The broker representing both may breach his fiduciary duty to one or both parties. For example, *X* is the broker representing *Y* in the sale of *Y's* house under a listing agreement. *X* also represents *P*, a prospective purchaser of a house under another agreement. *X* shows *P* the house owned by *Y*. *P* inquires whether the "asking" price is fair in light of the market conditions and the location of the property. *X* has a fiduciary duty to deal fairly with *P and Y*. *X* has a fiduciary duty to *Y* to obtain the best possible price according to the instructions given *X* by *Y*. This example illustrates conflict of interest when a broker represents more than one party to a transaction.

The law does not actually prohibit conflicts of interest. It prohibits a licensee from representing more than one party to a transaction without the knowledge and consent in writing of all parties for whom he acts. A licensee can act for more than one party if all parties for whom he acts know of the potential conflict of interest and all such parties give their consent in writing to the licensee's acting for those parties. The law does not specifically require the consent in writing to be prior to the licensee's acting for more than one party. However, a licensee would be well advised to require the consent to be made in writing before acting under a situation which results in a conflict of interest.

> (8) Placing a "for sale" or "for rent" sign on any property without the written consent of the owner, or his authorized agent.

This section prohibits the placing of a "for sale" or "for rent" sign upon any property without the owner's or his agent's permission in writing. Note that the broker does not have to have a listing agreement before the sign may be placed upon the property, merely the permission in writing from the owner. Nothing in the licensing law prohibits a broker from obtaining this permission from an owner even though the property may be listed with another broker.

> (9) Failing to voluntarily furnish a copy of any listing, sale, lease, or other contract relevant to a real estate transaction to all signatories thereof at the time of execution.

This subparagraph requires that the licensee voluntarily furnish to all signatories a copy of any contract relevant to a real estate transaction. The copy must be furnished *at the time of execution.* It is uncertain whether this subparagraph is intended to place an affirmative duty on the licensee to deliver copies to the signatories involved, or whether it prohibits a licensee from withholding a copy of a contract from a signatory after a request for such a copy has been made to the licensee. The most probable intention is to require the licensee to provide copies without a request from a signatory to the transaction. In cases when a wife and husband are signatories, the better practice would be to provide a copy to each even though they may have the same residence.

> (10) Failing to specify a definite termination date that is not subject to prior notice, in any listing contract.

This subparagraph has the effect of requiring that every listing contract have a definite expiration date and that the termination date be subject to prior notice. Open-ended listings would be prohibited under this subparagraph. Every listing contract would have to be for a definite term. At the expiration of the term there would be an automatic termination of the relationship created by the listing contract. The contract cannot include a provision which has the effect of extending the listing unless prior notice is given by either the broker or the client. Nothing in this section prohibits a broker from continuing a listing after the expiration of a prior listing, so long as there is a new agreement between the broker and the client and the new listing has a definite termination date which is not subject to prior notice.

For example, *X,* a licensed broker, entered into a listing contract with *S,* the seller of a residential property. The term of the listing is for ninety days. No sale is effected and the term expires. *X* obtains *S's* permission to continue the listing unless *S* gives *X* thirty days' notice of termination. This second agreement would violate the statute because the agreement does not have a definite termination date which is not subject to prior notice.

> (11) Inducing any party to a contract, sale or lease to break such contract for the purpose of substitution in lieu thereof of a new contract, where such substitution is motivated by the personal gain of the licensee.

This subparagraph prohibits interference by a licensee with a prior contractual relationship between two other parties in cases where the licensee is motivated by personal gain. For example, *X,* a licensed broker hears that *S,* the seller, and *B,* the buyer, have entered into a contract for the purchase and sale of *S's* house. *B* had previously contacted *X* in *B's* search of suitable property. A new property comes on the market, and *X* induces *B* to breach his contract with *S* and purchase the property from *Y*, for which *X* is entitled to a commission from *Y*. *X* would be in violation of the law.

Nothing in the licensing law prohibits a licensee from influencing a prospect to purchase or lease one property over another provided that no binding contract has been made. For example, *X* hears that *B* and *S* are about to enter into a contract for the purchase and sale of *S's* house. *S* has granted *B* an option to purchase. *X* contacts *B* and requests that he view *Y's* property. *B* does so and purchases *Y's* property. Even though *X* was motivated by personal gain from the commission realized on the sale by *Y* to *B*, there would be no violation because no prior contract was in existence.

(12) Accepting a commission or any valuable consideration by a salesperson or associate broker for the performance of any acts specified in this act, from any person, except the licensed real estate broker with whom he is affiliated.

This subparagraph applies only to salespersons and associate brokers and prohibits them from accepting a fee or commission for the performance of any act specified in the law from any person other than the employing broker. Any services performed by the salesperson must have been done within the scope of employment for the employing broker. Nothing prohibits a salesperson or associate broker from receiving a commission or fee for services performed, provided that the fee is received from the employing broker who is directly responsible to the commission for the supervision of the employee. For example, *X*, a licensed broker, employs *Y*, a licensed salesperson. *Y* is contacted by *B*, a buyer, about the property owned by *S*, who has listed that property with broker *Z*. Within the scope of his authority as an employee of *X*, *Y* contacts *Z* and ultimately arranges the sale of *S's* property to *B*. *Z* has agreed that *Y* would be entitled to share in the commission from *S*.

Z may not pay the commission to *Y* directly. *Z* must pay the commission to *X* as the employing broker of *Y*. If *X* wishes to pay over a portion of the commission to *Y*, *X* may do so. *Z* may not pay *Y* directly. *Y* may only work under the authority of *X* and is solely responsible to *X*.

(13) Failing to disclose to an owner in writing his intention or true position if he directly or indirectly through a third party, purchased for himself or acquires or intends to acquire any interest in or any option to purchase property which has been listed with his office to sell or lease.

This is a mandatory disclosure requirement. A broker must disclose *in writing* to the owner of property any direct or indirect interest that he may have in property listed with his office. That is, the broker who intends to directly or indirectly acquire an interest in property listed with his office must disclose this interest to the owner of the property. The interest of the broker in acquiring the property of a client raises conflict of interest between himself and the client. If the broker is acquiring an interest in the property either directly or indirectly, he may not be able to exercise independent judgment on behalf of the client because his interest is adverse to the client's. The regulation requires disclosure in writing to the client of the true interest of the broker. The client may then choose not to deal with the broker.

Note that the regulation does not prohibit a broker from having an interest in the purchase or lease of the property of his client. It merely requires disclosure. The requirement of disclosure extends to "indirect" as well as to "direct" interests. For example, *X*, a licensed broker, has a listing for the sale of *S's* property. A corporation of which *X* is a principal stockholder wishes to purchase *S's* property. Even though the corporation is a separate legal entity, as a principal owner of the corporation, *X* has an indirect interest and must disclose this interest to *S*. The law does not specify the time within which the disclosure must be made, but presumably disclosure would be effective only if it were made before the lease or purchase contract. If not, the law would afford no protection to the clients of licensed brokers.

(14) Being convicted in a court of competent jurisdiction of this or any other state, or Federal court, of forgery, embezzlement, obtaining money under false pretenses, bribery, larceny, extortion, conspiracy to defraud, or any similar offense or offenses, or pleading guilty or *nolo contendere* to any such offense or offenses.

This subparagraph makes it an offense to be convicted in any jurisdiction in the United States of certain crimes involving "moral turpitude." The offenses for which a license may be revoked include not only a conviction of the crime or crimes, but guilty pleas and pleas of *nolo contendere. Nolo contendere* pleas are those which a defendant pleads "no contest" to the charge. For purposes of criminal law, such a plea is considered to be a guilty plea. For purposes of civil law, the plea of *nolo contendere* is not considered an admission of guilt and the fact that a defendant has entered such a plea cannot be introduced in evidence at a civil trial. A guilty plea can be introduced against the defendant in a civil trial. Often, a defendant in a criminal case will seek to enter a plea of *nolo contendre* in order to plead "guilty" in criminal court, but will not admit guilt for purposes of a civil case brought by the person wronged by the defendant. In most cases the acceptance of a plea of *nolo contendere* is within the discretion of court in a criminal case.

Exhibit 13 lists the crimes enumerated in the subparagraph.

Exhibit 13
CRIMES LISTED IN SECTION 604(14)

- Forgery,
- Embezzlement,
- Obtaining money under false pretenses,
- Bribery,
- Larceny,
- Extortion,
- Conspiracy to defraud, and
- Any similar offense.

---

(15) Violating any rule or regulation promulgated by the commission in the interest of the public and consistent with the provisions of this act.

This subparagraph makes it a violation of the law to violate any rule promulgated by the commission.

(16) In the case of a broker licensee, failing to exercise adequate supervision over the activities of his licensed salespersons or associate brokers within the scope of this act.

A broker must exercise "adequate" supervision and control over salespersons and associate brokers. There is no objective standard for measuring "adequate" supervision as required by the law. Each case must depend on its own particular facts. If an employed associate broker or salesperson engages in a course of conduct of illegal activities over a period of time, this may be an indication that the broker is not providing adequate supervision. The longer the course of conduct and the more blatant the conduct, the more likely it is that the broker is failing in his duty to adequately supervise employees. Presumably, adequate supervision would include disciplining salespersons and associate brokers who violate either law or regulation.

(17) Failing, within a reasonable time as defined by the commission, to provide information requested by the commission as the result of a formal or informal complaint to the commission, which would indicate a violation of this act.

This subparagraph requires licensees to cooperate in administrative investigations initiated by the commission pursuant to its authority to discipline licensees. The failure to provide information is itself a violation. Since the administrative remedies of the commission are not "criminal" proceedings, the law compels cooperation. However, since the ultimate results of the commission's investigation may be penal in nature, it is possible that this section of the law violates the United States Constitution which protects an individual from being compelled to testify against himself.

Since the procedural requirements of "due process" are observed in the administrative as well as in the criminal procedure in Pennsylvania, it is likely that a violation of this particular subsection cannot be used against an individual licensee in investigation of his own case. However, this subparagraph could be used against a licensee to compel disclosure of information against another licensee or another individual. Since the constitutional guarantee of the Fifth Amendment applies only to the individual, one may be compelled to provide information against another under this subparagraph.

(18) Soliciting, selling or offering for sale real property by offering free lots, or conducting lotteries or contests or offering prizes for the purpose of influencing by deceptive conduct any purchaser or prospective purchaser of real property. The commission shall promulgate necessary rules and regulations to provide standards for nondeception conduct under this paragraph.

This subparagraph is designed to prevent the practice of promotions using "giveaways" as an inducement by deceptive conduct to influence purchasers of property. It seems clear that if a licensee were to offer a free lot as a prize for a drawing to people who visit a subdivision, this would be prohibited by the law. However, all cases are not so clear. For example, *X*, a licensee, offers free coffee and donuts or balloons for the children at a grand opening of a housing development. The coffee, donuts, and balloons are an inducement for people to come to the subdivision to see the houses and lots. It is clear that offering something does induce people to purchase. However, this technique is probably outside the scope of the law. However, if the licensee were to have a fishbowl full of marbles and asked people to guess the number, offering a pair of skis and a trip to Colorado as a prize, but with no intention by the broker to award the prize to a member of the public, this would be a promotional technique involving deceptive conduct that is prohibited by the law.

The subparagraph grants to the commission the authority to promulgate rules and regulations to provide standards for nondeceptive conduct.

(19) Paying or accepting, giving or charging any undisclosed commission, rebate, compensation or profit or expenditures for a principal, or in violation of this act.

This subparagraph deals with the practice of accepting or giving an unauthorized commission rebate or payment or expenditure for a principal. For example, *X*, a licensed broker, is manager of an apartment building owned by *Y*. *X* enters into an agreement with *Z's* company on behalf of *Y* to perform maintenance upon *Y's* apartment building. As an accommodation for giving *Z* the lucrative maintenance contract, *Z* pays *X* 10 percent of its earnings on the contract. Unless *X* discloses to *Y* the "kickback" received from *Z*, there would be a violation of the law.

Note that the law does not prohibit the payment of commissions, rebates, and compensation; it merely requires the disclosure of any such payments. Note also that nothing in this subparagraph prohibits splitting of commissions between brokers, so long as the payment is pursuant to an agreement between the broker and the principal. In such cases, the commission is disclosed in the original listing agreement.

(20) Any conduct in a real estate transaction which demonstrates bad faith, dishonesty, untrustworthiness, or incompetency.

This subparagraph covers many situations involving dishonesty, bad faith, untrustworthiness or incompetency. None of these terms is given a precise definition in the law. However, it may be assumed that when conduct by a licensee is dishonest, untrustworthy, or incompetent, or if the licensee demonstrates bad faith and as a result of this conduct a third party is damaged, then there would be violation of this subparagraph. For example, *X*, a licensed broker, has a listing to sell *Y's* house. *X* receives from *B* an offer to purchase *Y's* house. Rather than require *B* to sign a written contract, *X* takes *B's* word that *B* will purchase the property. *B* does not make an earnest money deposit to secure his promise to perform the contract. At the time and place of settlement, *B* refuses to complete the purchase on grounds that there is no written contract as required by the state's statute of frauds. *Y* has sustained damages for out-of-pocket expenses and is forced to sell the property at a lower price to another buyer. Under these circumstances, the loss sustained by *Y* was a direct result of *Y's* being unable to enforce the contract between *Y* and *B*. Since *X* knew, or reasonably should have known, that a written contract was required, *X* did not meet the standard of care and competency required for brokers. *X* would be in violation of this subparagraph.

Another example of bad faith, dishonesty, and untrustworthiness is where *X*, a licensed broker, has a listing on a house owned by *S*, the seller. The house is listed at $75,000 which is the fair market value of the property. *B*, a buyer, approaches *X* and says that he will pay $65,000 for the property, $10,000 less than the fair market value. *X* tells *S* that $65,000 is a fair price for the property and urges *S* to accept the offer even though *X* knows that the fair market value is higher. A contract is executed between *S* and *B*. The day following settlement, *B* resells the property for $75,000. Under these circumstances, the conduct of *X* demonstrates bad faith, dishonesty, and untrustworthiness.

The key elements in determining whether the conduct is prohibited by law is whether the licensee has not met the level of honesty, competency, and trustworthiness required of the profession. If an innocent party is damaged by the conduct, it is more likely that the conduct would be considered to be a violation of the law.

(21) Performing any act for which an appropriate real estate license is required and is not currently in effect.

This subparagraph applies to licensees and nonlicensees. For example, it prohibits a salesperson licensee from performing acts which are limited to brokers. Rental listing referral agents cannot perform the services of salespersons. Limited brokers cannot perform all of the activities of a broker. This subparagraph limits a licensee's activities to those not prohibited by the licensing law. Note that a broker has authority to perform all activities of any of the other licensees. This subparagraph also prohibits brokerage activities by licensees whose licenses are not current.

(22) Violating any provision of the Act of October 27, 1955 (P.L. 744, No. 222), known as the "Pennsylvania Human Relations Act," or any order or consent decree of the Pennsylvania Human Relations Commission issued pursuant to such act if such order of consent decree resulted from a complaint of discrimination in the area of activities authorized by virtue of this act. Such activities include but are not limited to:

(i) Accepting listings on the understanding that illegal discrimination in the sale or rental of housing is to be practiced due to race, color, religious creed, sex, ancestry, national origin, physical handicap, disability, or use of a guide dog because of blindness of user of a prospective lessee or purchaser.

(ii) Giving false information for purposes of discrimination in the rental or sale of housing due to race, color, religious creed, sex, ancestry, national origin, physical handicap, disability, or use of a guide dog because of blindness of user of a prospective lessee or purchaser.

(iii) Making distinctions in locations of housing or dates of availability of housing for purposes of discrimination in the rental or sale of such housing due to race, color, religious creed, sex, ancestry, national origin, physical handicap, disability, or use of a guide dog because of blindness of user of the prospective lessee or purchaser.

Nothing contained in paragraph (22) is intended to preclude the State Real Estate Commission from conducting its own investigation and maintaining its own file on any complaint of discrimination. The intent hereunder is to allow the Pennsylvania Human Relations Commission a reasonable period of time to conduct its own investigations, hold hearings, render its decisions and inform the Pennsylvania Real Estate Commission of its findings prior to the State Real Estate Commission taking action against any broker, salesperson or sales associate charged with a violation of paragraph (22).

If in the event the Pennsylvania Human Relations Commission does not act on a discrimination complaint within 90 days after it is filed with the Pennsylvania Human Relations Commission then the State Real Estate Commission may proceed with action against such licensee.

The 90-day waiting period delaying State Real Estate Commission action against licensee accused of discrimination applies only in initial complaints against such licensee, second or subsequent complaints may be brought by individuals or the Pennsylvania Human Relations Commission directly to the State Real Estate Commission.

Subparagraph (22) deals with violation of the Pennsylvania Human Relations Act. The act prohibits illegal discrimination practiced due to race, color, religion, creed, sex, ancestry, or national origin. The purpose of this subparagraph is to give primary jurisdiction to investigate complaints against licensees to the Pennsylvania Human Relations Commission. If the Human Relations Commission enters an order against a licensee which is subsequently violated, or if the licensee does not abide by the terms and conditions of a consent order entered by the commission, the licensee violates subparagraph (22). Those activities which would violate an order or consent decree are those listed in subsections (i), (ii), and (iii).

Subsection (i) prohibits the acceptance of listings upon the understanding that illegal discrimination is to be practiced in the sale or rental of housing, and subsection (ii) prohibits the giving of false information for the purpose of illegally discriminating. For example, *X*, a licensed broker, advises *B*, a potential buyer of property, that there is no property for sale in a certain subdivision, when *X* knows that there is property for sale there but that there is a preference on the part of the seller and his neighbors that the property not be sold to members of *B's* race. Both (i) and (ii) would be violated.

Subparagraph (iii) prohibits the practice of "steering" purchasers or lessees into certain geographical locations in order to maintain racial, ethnic, or religious homogenity of neighborhoods. A licensee cannot make any distinction based upon illegal discrimination in location of housing.

Note that the discrimination prohibited is *illegal* discrimination. It would not be a violation of this subparagraph to discriminate on the basis of economic status, marital status, or age. For example, if licensee broker were not to disclose the location of available housing in a high-priced housing development to a potential buyer of very modest means, this would probably not be illegal discrimination. However, such discrimination may be interpreted as illegal discrimination if the buyer is also a member of a class protected by the Human Relations Act.

The subsection also details the procedure for cooperation between the Human Relations Commission and the Real Estate Commission in investigating complaints of discrimination by licensees. The Human Relations Commission has a "reasonable" amount of time to investigate, hold hearings, render decisions, and report to the Real Estate Commission. If the Human Relations Commission does not act within ninety days after a complaint has been filed, the Real Estate Commission may proceed against a licensee for illegal discrimination. After the first complaint against a licensee, the Real Estate Commission may proceed against a licensee without having to await action by the Human Relations Commission.

Exhibits 14 and 15 summarize the mandatory duties and prohibited acts under Section 604.

Section 605. Out-of-state land sales — approval. Any person who proposes to engage in sales of a promotional nature in this Commonwealth for a property located outside of this Commonwealth, shall first apply to the commission for its approval before so doing, and they and their salesmen shall comply with such rules, regulations, restrictions and conditions pertaining thereto as the commission may impose as well as all those provisions set forth in this act.

This section requires prior approval of the commission before a person may engage in sales of a "promotional" nature of lands outside the commonwealth. This section is designed to control the practice of selling interests in real property at parties and through mass media promotional techniques. The Real Estate Commission may pass rules, regulations and restrictions in order to control promotional techniques of out-of-state land sales within Pennsylvania.

The section requires salespersons to comply with any rules and regulations of the commission that may be imposed upon such promotional techniques.

Exhibit 14
MANDATORY DUTIES UNDER SECTION 604

Of *All* Licensees

- Furnish voluntarily copies of documents to all signatories at the time of execution [¶ 9],
- Specify a definite termination date in listing contracts [¶ 10],
- Disclose true position if there is an intent to acquire a direct or indirect interest in listed property [¶ 13], and
- Provide information requested by the commission in aid of its investigations [¶ 17].

Of Brokers and Limited Brokers

- Retain deposits and monies pending consummation or termination of the transaction [¶ 5(i)],
- Account to parties for full amounts of monies deposited [¶ 5(i)],
- Deposit immediately funds of offers in custodial or trust account [¶ 5(iv)],
- Keep records of all funds deposited in trust or custodial account [¶ 5(v)],
- Make trust or custodial accounts available for inspection by commission upon demand [¶ 5(v)],
- Preserve records relating to a transaction for three years following its consummation [¶ 6], and
- Supervise and control salespersons and associate brokers [¶ 6].

Of Salespersons, Limited Salespersons, and Associate Brokers

- Pay over promptly all deposits to their broker [¶ 5(ii)].

Exhibit 15
PROHIBITED ACTS UNDER SECTION 604

For *All* Licensees

- Making a substantial misrepresentation [¶ 1],
- Making a false promise likely to influence others [¶ 2],
- Misleading or false advertising [¶ 3],
- Using trade name or insignia of trade organizations when not entitled to do so [¶ 3],
- Acting for more than one party to a transaction without the knowledge and consent in writing of all parties [¶ 7],
- Placing a "for sale" or "for rent" sign on property without permission [¶ 8],
- Inducing a party to breach a contract for the personal gain of the licensee [¶ 11],
- Being convicted of crimes involving moral turpitude [¶ 14],
- Violating any rule or regulation of the commission [¶ 15],
- Paying or accepting an undisclosed commission or rebate [¶ 19],
- Engaging in conduct which demonstrates bad faith, dishonesty, untrustworthiness, or incompetency [¶ 20],
- Performing any act for which a license is required [¶ 21],
- Violating an order or consent decree of the Pennsylvania Human Relations Commission [¶ 22],
- Accepting a listing with the understanding that illegal discrimination is to be practiced [¶ 22(i)],
- Giving false information for the purpose of illegally discriminating [¶ 22(ii)], and
- Making distinctions in location or dates of availability for the purpose of illegal discrimination [¶ 22(iii)].

For Brokers and Limited Brokers

- Making a misrepresentation or false promises through salespersons, associate brokers, or others [¶ 3],
- Commingling money or property of others with his own funds [¶ 5(iii)],
- Making payment in advance of any trust funds [¶ 5(iv)].

For Salespersons, Limited Salespersons, and Associate Brokers

- Accepting a commission or other valuable consideration from anyone other than the employing broker [¶ 12].

CHAPTER 7.
PROCEEDINGS BEFORE THE COMMISSION

Section 701. Hearings held by commission.

(a) The said hearings may be held by the commission or any members thereof, or by any of its duly authorized representatives, or by any other person duly authorized by the commission for such purpose in any particular case.

(b) The commission may adopt the findings in the report or may, with or without additional testimony, either return the matter to the representative for such further consideration as the commission deems necessary or make additional or other findings of fact on the basis of all the legally probative evidence in the record and enter its conclusions of law and order in accordance with the requirements for the issuance of an adjudication under 2 Pa.C.S. § 103, known as the Administrative Agency Law.

(c) Proceedings before the commission shall be conducted in accordance with Title 1, Part 2 of the Pennsylvania Code.

Section 702. Imputed knowledge, limitations. No violation of any of the provisions of this act on the part of any salesperson, associate broker, or other employee of any licensed broker, shall be grounds for the revocation or suspension of the license of the employer of such salesperson, associate broker, or employee, unless it shall appear upon the hearings held, that such employer had actual knowledge of such violation. A course of dealing shown to have been followed by such employee shall constitute prima facie evidence of such knowledge upon the part of his employer.

This section limits the liability for suspension or revocation of the license of an employing broker for acts of his salespersons, associate brokers, or other employees. Knowledge of the illegal acts of employees will not be imputed. "Imputed knowledge" is that knowledge of a fact which a person is presumed at law to have because of a certain relationship between that person and another who actually knows the fact in question. Imputed knowledge is sometimes referred to as *"presumed knowledge."* This situation commonly arises when an employee knows a fact and, because the employee knows, the employer is presumed to know. For example, *X* is an employee of a retail business engaged in the sale of fruits and vegetables. *O* is the owner of the establishment. A customer tells *X* that there is a banana peel on the floor. *X* does not report this fact to *O*, nor does *X* remove the banana peel. A short time later, *P*, a patron, is injured when he slipped on the banana peel. In a claim brought in court by *P* against *O*, it could be argued that *O* knew about the presence of the banana peel through his employee, *X*. The knowledge of the fact of the banana peel's presence on the floor is imputed to *O* through his employee, *X*.

This section of the law specifically limits imputed knowledge of an employing broker for the acts of his salespersons, associate brokers, and other employees. However, there are two situations when the limitation does not apply. Upon a hearing of the case against an employee of a licensed broker, if it should appear that the broker had guilty knowledge of such activities of employees, then the limitation would not apply. In addition, if the employee engaged in the illegal course of conduct over a period of time, the employing broker is presumed to have actual knowledge because of the continuous nature of the employee's activities. This would apply when the employing broker *should have known* of the illegal activities of employees whether or not he actually had known of the acts.

The law makes specific reference to *prima facie* evidence of a broker's knowledge of the illegal acts of his employees in cases where there is a course of illegal dealing. *Prima facie* evidence means that the broker has the burden of proving that he did *not* have knowledge. In most other situations, the complaining party has the burden of proving that the broker *did* have knowledge. Of course, if a broker can prove that he did not have actual knowledge of an illegal course of conduct of his employees, the broker may still be guilty of failing to adequately supervise the employees, as required by Section 604(16).

CHAPTER 8.
REAL ESTATE RECOVERY FUND

Chapter 8 deals with the Real Estate Recovery Fund. This is a fund which is established to assist parties who have been monetarily damaged by the wrongful acts of licensees and have no recourse against the licensee himself. This chapter of the law details the establishment, funding, and operation of the Real Estate Recovery Fund.

Section 801. Establishment of the fund. There is hereby established the Real Estate Recovery Fund for the purposes hereinafter set forth in this act.

Section 801 establishes the Fund.

Section 802. Funding of the fund. Each licensee entitled to renew his license on or after February 28, 1980, shall, when so renewing his license pay in addition to the applicable license fee a further fee of $10, which shall be paid and credited to the Real Estate Recovery Fund, thereafter any person upon receiving his initial real estate license, shall, in addition to all fees, pay into the Real Estate Recovery Fund a sum of $10. If at the commencement of any biennial renewal period beginning in 1982 and thereafter, the balance of the fund is less than $300,000, the commission may assess an additional fee, in addition to the renewal fee, against each licensee in an amount not to exceed $10 which will yield revenues sufficient to bring the balance of the fund to $500,000. All said fees shall be paid into the State Treasury and credited to the Real Estate Recovery Fund, and said deposits shall be allocated solely for the purposes of the fund as provided in this act. The fund shall be invested and interest/dividends shall accrue to the fund.

This section provides for funding of the Recovery Fund. Each current licensee shall pay to the fund the sum of $10 at the time of the next annual renewal following February 28, 1980. When an individual becomes licensed for the first time, as part of the fees paid for licensing, he shall contribute $10 toward the fund. There is a provision for additional assessment if the fund does not have a balance of $500,000. The funds are to be invested with all interests and dividends accruing to the fund.

Section 803. Application for recovery from fund.

(a) When any aggrieved person obtains a final judgment in any court of competent jurisdiction against any person licensed under this act, upon grounds of fraud, misrepresentation or deceit with reference to any transaction for which a license is required under this act and which cause of action occurred on or after the effective date of this act, the aggrieved person may, upon termination of all proceedings, including reviews and appeals, file an application in the court in which the judgment was entered for an order directing payment out of the Real Estate Recovery Fund of the amount unpaid upon the judgment.

(b) The aggrieved person shall be required to show:

(1) That he is not a spouse of the debtor, or the personal representative of said spouse.

(2) That he has obtained a final judgment as set out in this section.

(3) That all reasonable personal acts, rights of discovery and such other remedies at law and in equity as exist have been exhausted in the collection thereof.

(4) That he is making said application no more than one year after the termination of the proceedings, including reviews and appeals in connection with the judgment.

Subsection (a) requires an applicant for recovery from the fund to obtain a final judgment against a licensee on grounds of fraud, misrepresentation, or deceit. In addition, the applicant must show that he is not the spouse of the debtor, that a final judgment has been obtained, that the applicant has exhausted all remedies at law or in equity against the licensee and has been unable to collect the judgment, and that no longer than one year has elapsed from the time of the termination of proceedings including appeals. If the applicant can show all of these, then he may be entitled to receive money from the fund.

Subsection (b) prescribes the prerequisites for a claim against the Real Estate Recovery Fund. Note that the claimant must meet all the requirements; there is no provision for a waiver of any requirement.

(c) The commission shall have the right to answer actions provided for under this section, and subject to court approval, it may compromise a claim based upon the application of the aggrieved party.

(d) When there is an order of the court to make payment or a claim is otherwise to be levied against the fund, such amount shall be paid to the claimant in accordance with the limitations contained in this section. Notwithstanding any other provisions of this section, the liability of that portion of the fund allocated for the purpose of this act shall not exceed $20,000 for any one judgment. If the $20,000 liability of the Real Estate Recovery Fund as provided herein is insufficient to pay in full claims adjudicated valid of all aggrieved persons against any one licensee, such $20,000 shall be distributed among them in such ratio that the respective claims of the aggrieved applicants bear to the aggregate of such claims held valid. If, at any time, the money deposited in the Real Estate Recovery Fund is insufficient to satisfy any duly authorized claim or portion thereof, the commission shall, when sufficient money has been deposited in the fund, satisfy such unpaid claims or portions thereof, in the order that such claims or portions thereof were originally filed, plus accumulated interest at the rate of 6% a year.

These subsections give the commission the authority to defend a claim against the fund and to compromise the claim of the aggrieved party. The maximum amount that can be claimed from the Recovery Fund per licensee is $20,000 per judgment. Note that this is regardless of the number of claimants to each judgment. For example, if one licensee were to cause the loss to 100 claimants, each of whom obtain judgment in one lawsuit, the total maximum recoverable for *all* claimants is $20,000. The subsection provides for proration of the available funds in accordance with the portion of the total loss born by each claimant or aggrieved party. In the example, if each of the 100 claimants sustained a loss of $1,000 because of the conduct of one licensee, then each would be entitled to receive $200 from the fund.

Subsection (d) further provides that if the total fund is insufficient to pay all claims, then as the fund is built, payment will be made to claimants on a first-come, first-served basis. Note that there is provision for the payment of interest at the rate of 6 percent on funds due and owing claimants.

(e) Upon petition of the commission the court may require all claimants and prospective claimants against one licensee to be joined in one action, to the end that the respective rights of all such claimants to the Real Estate Recovery Fund may be equitably adjudicated and settled.

This subsection provides that the claims of several claimants against a licensee may be consolidated so that all claims for recovery from the fund may be heard in one law suit.

(f) Should the commission pay from the Real Estate Recovery Fund any amount in settlement of a claim as provided for in this act against a licensee, the license of that person shall automatically suspend upon the effective date of the payment thereof by the commission. No such licensee shall be granted reinstatement until he has repaid in full plus interest at the rate of 6% a year, the amount paid from the Real Estate Recovery Fund.

This section requires that a licensee who had had recovery from the fund obtained by claimants because of his wrongful act shall automatically have his license suspended. He is not entitled to have a reinstatement of his license until all funds together with interest have been repaid to the fund.

Exhibit 16 summarizes the provisions for recovery from the Real Estate Recovery Fund.

Exhibit 16
PROVISIONS FOR RECOVERY FROM THE REAL ESTATE RECOVERY FUND

The claimant must

- Obtain a final judgment against a licensee based upon fraud, misrepresentation or deceit,
- Exhaust all remedies at law or in equity and have no success collecting from the licensee,
- Make application no longer than one year after the termination of proceeding in court,
- Not be the spouse of the licensee or the personal representative of the spouse of the licensee, and
- Limit his claim to a maximum of $20,000.

CHAPTER 9.
REPEALER AND EFFECTIVE DATE

Section 901. Repealer. The act of May 1, 1929 (P.L. 1216, No. 427), known as the "Real Estate Brokers License Act of one thousand nine hundred and twenty-nine," is repealed to the following conditions:

(1) All valid licenses issued prior to the effective date of this act under the provisions of said 1929 Act shall continue with full force and validity during the period for which issued. For the subsequent license period, and each license period thereafter, the commission shall renew such licenses without requiring any license examination to be taken: provided, however, that applicants for renewal or holders of such licenses shall be subject to all other provisions of this act.

(2) All proceedings in progress on the effective date shall continue to proceed under the terms of the act under which they were brought.

(3) All offenses alleged to have occurred prior to the effective date of this act shall be processed under the act of May 1, 1929 (P.L. 1216, No. 427).

Chapter 9, and in particular Section 901, establishes the procedure for phasing in the new law. The old law is formally repealed. All proceedings under the old law are to continue under the old law and offenses committed under the old law will be processed under the old law. All licenses issued under the old law are presumed to meet the requirements of the new law, all licensees are subject to the new law but no licensee is required to be reexamined.

Section 902. Effective date. Section 561 shall take effect September 1, 1980 and the remaining provisions of this act shall take effect immediately.

The law had an immediate effective date, except for the provision (Section 561) relating to the licensing of rental listing referral agents which has an effective date of September 1, 1980. The purpose for the delay in the effective date of the provision requiring licenses of rental listing referral agents was to permit those engaged as owners or managers of rental listing referral agencies to have an opportunity to meet the requirements of licensure.

PART III

Preparing for the Examination

There are thirty questions on the "state" or license law portion of the examination. These questions deal exclusively with the Pennsylvania real estate licensing and follow the structure of the "uniform" portion of the examination. The questions are multiple choice in two formats. The first type supplies four different responses to an incomplete sentence. The following is an example of this format:

Example 1

An associate broker is

A. A licensed broker employed by another broker.
B. A broker of record who has associated with another broker of record.
C. A broker under a multiple-listing arrangement.
D. None of the above.

The examinee is to choose from among the responses the word or phrase which best completes the sentence or concept. If none of the offered responses best completes the sentence or concept, then "none of the above" is the appropriate response. One method of answering this type question is to read the phrase with each response, as follows:

A. An associate broker is a licensed broker employed by another broker.
B. An associate broker is a broker of record who has associated with another broker of record.
C. An associate broker is a broker under a multiple-listing arrangement.

Since the response A above is the statutory definition of associate broker, it is the proper response. Remember, even if one response seems more correct than the others upon first reading, it is still wise to read each response separately. Often, reading the entire sentence or concept places a response in a different light than if read separately.

The second format presents two possibilities. The examinee must apply each possibility to the question given and respond to one of four alternatives offered. Under most circumstances, the two possibilities will not be alternatives. That is, applying one response will not automatically exclude the other. Rather, each of the two responses may apply to the question, or both or neither will apply. The following is an example of this format:

Example 2

As defined by the licensing law, what does the term "real estate" include?

I. Land within Pennsylvania.
II. Land outside Pennsylvania.

A. I only.
B. II only.
C. Both I and II.
D. Neither I nor II.

This latter format requires an understanding of the statement and each possibility offered. Each possibility should be read separately with the statement offered. In example 2, the statement should be read as follows:

As defined by the licensing law, the term "real estate" includes land within Pennsylvania.

As defined by the licensing law, the term "real estate" includes land outside Pennsylvania.

Section 201 defines real estate as including land within Pennsylvania and elsewhere. Therefore, both possibilities are true. The next step is to choose the correct response from those offered, which, in this example, would be C, "Both I and II."

With the format offering two possibilities, the responses offered will always be the same and be given in the same sequence. Most questions using the first format will include a response such as "None of the above" or "All of the above." These responses will usually appear as letter "D" among the responses offered.

The first step in answering any question is to clearly understand the question. This is essential to choosing the correct answer. In certain cases, facts may be introduced into a question which have no bearing on the question and are inserted to test the examinee's ability to eliminate facts or concepts not part of the problem. This type of question is most common when a factual situation is presented. The following is an example:

Example 3

X, a licensed broker, employs *Y* as a salesperson. *Y* works in a branch office under the supervision and control of *Z*, an associate broker. *Y* wishes to change employers. What must *Y* do?

I. Notify the commission in writing, return the pocket card, pay the required fee.
II. Obtain the permission in writing of *X*.

A. I only.
B. II only.
C. Both I and II.
D. Neither I nor II.

In example 3, the question asked is: "What must *Y* do if he wishes to change employers?" However, the question presents a trap for the unwary examinee. Both *X*, the employing broker, and *Z*, the associate broker, are mentioned in the facts presented. The examinee may believe that the question requires a choice between the employing broker and the supervising broker. Since *X* is the broker of record, *X* bears ultimate responsibility to the commission for *Y*. It must be *X* who is required to take appropriate action on behalf of *Y*. Therefore the response which mentions *X* must be the correct response. The examinee who falls into the trap will answer the question incorrectly. Under Section 603, the former employing broker is not required to give written permission for a salesperson to change employers. The correct response is A. I only. II, which makes reference to *X*, is designed to make use of facts which have no bearing on the correct answer.

Remember that the best way to answer a question is to understand the "call" of the question, and choose the response or responses which answer the question. Do not be misled by extraneous facts.

It is important not to read too much into a question. Often more than one answer may, under remote circumstances, seem to apply to the question presented. In such cases, for questions using the first format always choose the *best* answer. In questions using the second format where two responses to a question may be possible, when in doubt choose both unless one of the responses would only apply under very remote circumstances. The following is an example of this situation:

Example 4

X is a licensed broker who has failed to renew his license. Under applicable law, pending renewal of the license, what may *X* not do?

I. Employ an associate broker to perform brokerage activities.
II. Perform any of the activities of a broker.

A. I only.
B. II only.
C. Both I and II.
D. Neither I nor II.

It seems clear that if a broker has not renewed his license he has no authority to hire an associate broker to perform brokerage activities since, by definition, an associate broker is employed by a *broker*. Response I would be correct. Since a broker's license is required prior to performing brokerage activities (Section 201), response II would also seem to be correct. However, if the broker were an attorney-at-law, a court-appointed fiduciary, the owner of property, or were exempt for some other reason, the failure to renew the broker's license would not bar *X* from performing activities listed in Section 201. Therefore, as an *absolute* certainty response, II cannot be chosen. However, since the facts do not indicate that *X* would be otherwise exempt, and since under normal circumstances the failure to renew a license is a bar to engaging in activities of a broker, II should also be chosen as a response. The proper answer to example 5 is C. Both I and II.

If the question has been read carefully and the "call" of the question is understood, many examinees find that their first impressions as to the correct answer should be trusted. Often, rereading the question leads to confusion. If an answer is not immediately known, the question should be set aside to be considered later. Often, a subsequent question or answer will jog the memory and provide a clue about the correct answer to the question which was deferred. However, when setting aside a question on the examination be sure to make an identifying mark on the question booklet *not* on the answer sheet. A stray mark on the machine-graded answer sheet might be interpreted as a response and be scored as an incorrect answer.

There is no penalty for guessing. An incorrect answer which is the product of a guess is scored the same as a carefully considered incorrect answer. Since there are only four possible responses, there is a 25 percent probability of guessing the correct answer. Often, it is possible to eliminate one or more responses as not being correct. This increases the probability of a successful guess. The probability might also be increased by keeping in mind the purposes of the real estate licensing law. If one response is more in keeping with the general objectives of regulating real estate practice and protecting the public interest, it is more probable that that answer is correct. The following summarizes the procedure for answering the questions:

- Read the question carefully.
- Understand the "call" of the question.
- Read each response carefully.
- Apply each response to the question asked.
- Choose the correct response and mark on answer sheet.

If the answer is not immediately known,

- Defer answering, continue with examination, then return, and/or
- Eliminate known wrong responses, choose or guess among remaining possible responses, mark on answer sheet.

SAMPLE QUESTIONS

The following questions are samples based upon the licensing law. After each question is the correct answer together with a brief explanation and the citation to the applicable section in the licensing law.

1. A license as a rental listing referral agent is required for

   A. The person who performs the service.
   B. The owner of the rental units.
   C. The owner or manager of the rental listing referral agency.
   D. None of the above.

Answer C. The owner or manager is required to be licensed [§201].

2. Who may engage in the sale of cemetery lots for a commission or fee?
   I. Limited broker.
   II. Broker.

   A. I only.
   B. II only.
   C. Both I and II.
   D. Neither I nor II.

Answer C. Both I and II. A broker may engage in any activity that a limited broker may do; however, the reverse is not true, the limited broker's activities being limited by statute [§201].

3. In what circumstances may recovery be denied under the licensing law in a civil suit for real estate brokerage commission for services performed for another?
   I. The person seeking recovery was duly licensed at the time brokerage services were performed but not at the time the services were offered.
   II. The person seeking recovery was duly registered at the time services were performed but not at the time the services were offered.

A. I only.
B. II only.
C. Both I and II.
D. Neither I nor II.

Answer D. Both I and II. The person seeking recovery must have been licensed at the time the services were offered [§302].

4. Which of the following is *not* considered a school within the licensing law?

A. A private real estate school.
B. An individual who conducts classes for others in his own home, whether or not a fee is charged.
C. A university accredited by the Middle States Association of Colleges and Secondary Schools, which conducts classes in real estate.
D. None of the above.

Answer C. An accredited university is not considered as a "school" for purposes of the licensing act [§201].

5. What penalty may be assessed against a person upon the first conviction of violation of the provisions of the licensing act?
I. Payment of a fine of not less than $100 nor more than $500.
II. Imprisonment not to exceed three months.

A. I only.
B. II only.
C. Both I and II.
D. Neither I nor II.

Answer B. II only. The law does not establish a minimum fine, only a maximum fine of $500 [§203].

6. *X* and *Y* are neighbors, owners of lots 1 and 2, respectively, in Jonathan Acres subdivision. Neither is licensed under the licensing law. Each wishes to sell his lot. *X* knows that *A* is interested in buying lot 2. *Y* knows that *B* is interested in buying lot 1. *X* and *Y* agree that each shall arrange the sale of the other's lot; however, they agree that neither shall be required to pay the other a fee or commission. Both properties are sold as agreed. *X* and *Y*

A. Would be exempt from licensure as owners of the properties sold.
B. Would be exempt from licensure because no fees or commissions were paid.
C. Are not exempt and are in violation of the licensing law.
D. None of the above.

Answer C. Neither *X* nor *Y* was owner of the lot sold for the other. The "owner" exemption does not apply. Even though no money changed hands for brokerage services, they agreed to exchange services which constitutes consideration. Both *X* and *Y* are in violation of the license law [§ §201 and 304].

7. In order for a nonlicensed person to act for another as attorney-in-fact and be exempt from licensure,

A. The services cannot be rendered for a fee or commission.
B. The power of attorney must be recorded with the Real Estate Commission.
C. The attorney-in-fact must be related to the person for whom the services are rendered.
D. None of the above.

Answer D. None of the above. The services may be performed for a fee. The power must be recorded in the county where the property is located and there is no requirement that the attorney-in-fact be related to the person for whom the services are performed [§304].

8. For whom would the exemption from licensure apply for the sale of corporate owned real property?
   I. Licensees in the employ of the corporation.
   II. All officers of the corporation actively engaged in the sale of corporate property.

   A. I only.
   B. II only.
   C. Both I and II.
   D. Neither I nor II.

Answer D. Neither I nor II. A licensee needs no exemption. The exemption applies to only five officers of the corporation, not only to those actively engaged in sale of corporate real property [§304].

9. The Pennsylvania Real Estate Commission *does not* have the statutory authority to

   A. Approve schools.
   B. Examine applicants.
   C. Issue licenses.
   D. The commission has authority to do all of the above.

Answer C. The Department of State, Commissioner of Professional and Occupational Affairs has authority to issue licenses [§401].

10. The applicant for a broker's license must first

   A. Meet the qualifications for licensure.
   B. Take the examination and score a passing grade.
   C. Be duly registered.
   D. None of the above.

Answer A. The applicant must meet the qualifications for licensure [§511].

11. After passing the examination, the application for licensure as a broker must be submitted

   A. Within three years of the date within which the applicant passed the examination.
   B. As soon as possible.
   C. As soon as the applicant has completed his three-year apprenticeship.
   D. None of the above.

Answer D. None of the above. The application must be submitted within three years after *taking* the examination [§512(d)].

12. Which of the following is *not* a requirement for licensure as a salesperson?
   I. 18 years of age, take and pass the written examination.
   II. Six semester credit hours of 15 hours each in approved real estate instruction.

   A. I only.
   B. II only.
   C. Both I and II.
   D. Neither I nor II.

Answer A. I only. The educational requirements are four semester credit hours at 15 hours each [§521(2)].

13. The application for a license as salesperson shall be made in writing and shall include

    A. A sworn statement by a licensed broker certifying the reputation of the applicant.
    B. Two photographs.
    C. Transcript of courses taken.
    D. None of the above.

Answer D. None of the above. The sworn statement is required to be from the employing broker certifying that the broker will actively supervise and train the salesperson [§522(b)].

14. If the applicant for a broker's license is a corporation, to whom do the requirements for licensure as to reputation apply?
    I. The individual designated as broker of record.
    II. All officers of the corporation.

    A. I only.
    B. II only.
    C. Both I and II.
    D. Neither I nor II.

Answer A. I only. The requirements of reputation do not apply to the designated broker of record and others engaged in the real estate business [§513].

15. How must the applicant for limited salesperson qualify for licensure?
    I. He must meet the educational requirements.
    II. He must take and pass the limited salesperson examination.

    A. I only.
    B. II only.
    C. Both I and II.
    D. Neither I nor II.

Answer D. Neither I nor II. The only qualification is that the applicant be 18 years of age and have a good reputation [§§501, 541].

16. The following is *not* a qualification for builder-owner salesperson's license:

    A. Take and score a passing grade on the builder-owner salesperson's examination.
    B. Be at least 18 years of age.
    C. Be employed by a "builder-owner" as defined by the law.
    D. None of the above.

Answer A. The builder-owner salesperson must take the *standard* salesperson examination. There is no separate examination for builder-owner salesperson [§551].

17. What must the applicant for rental listing referral agent do in order to be licensed?
    I. Meet all the qualifications for a salesperson's license.
    II. Make application in the same manner as a salesperson.

    A. I only.
    B. II only.
    C. Both I and II.
    D. Neither I nor II.

Answer A. I only. The rental listing referral agent need not have a sponsoring broker [§§561 and 521].

18. All brokers who do business in Pennsylvania are required to

A. Maintain an office at a fixed location approved by the commission.
B. Hire associate brokers.
C. Have at least one salesperson employed.
D. None of the above.

Answer D. None of the above. Only resident brokers are required to maintain an office at a fixed location approved by the commission [§§601(a), 602(b)].

19. An associate broker

A. May not be employed by more than one broker.
B. May have his own branch office licensed in his name.
C. May do anything a broker can do.
D. None of the above.

Answer A. An associate broker may be employed by only one broker, though the associate broker may perform services for more than one, as for example under a multiple-listing arrangement [§603]. An associate broker can manage a branch office, but cannot have it licensed in his or her name [§601], nor can the associate broker do everything a broker can do.

20. To whom are nonresident licenses granted?
I. To brokers and salespersons who are duly licensed in their own state.
II. To brokers and salespersons who do not maintain a place of business within Pennsylvania.

A. I only.
B. II only.
C. Both I and II.
D. Neither I nor II.

Answer A. I only. The nonresident broker provision is intended to permit brokers in "reciprocal" states from having to comply with Pennsylvania application procedures. They are exempt from maintaining a fixed place of business in Pennsylvania, although they may maintain one if they so choose [§602(b)].

21. If a licensee wishes to change employing brokers, he

A. Must immediately notify the commission in writing within ten days after the change.
B. Have the former broker return the licensee's pocket card.
C. Pay the required fee.
D. None of the above.

Answer C. The licensee must notify the commission 10 days prior to the intended change, pay the required fee, and return his or her pocket card [§603].

22. Under what circumstances may the Real Estate Commission initiate an investigation of a licensee?
I. Upon a verified complaint in writing from any person.
II. Upon its own motion.

A. I only.
B. II only.
C. Both I and II.
D. Neither I nor II.

Answer C. Both I and II. The commission may investigate with or without a specific complaint [§604].

X, a licensed salesperson, employed by *Y*, a licensed broker, advises *B*, the buyer of a building lot, that the lot has been approved for an "on site" sewage disposal system. The lot has not been approved. *B* buys the lot and finds that the lot has not been approved. The proper authority conducts the inspection at no cost to *B* and approves the lot for "on site" sewage.

23. In the above example, *X* would be guilty of

A. Pursuing a continued and flagrant course of misrepresentation.
B. Misleading or untruthful advertising.
C. Making a substantial misrepresentation.
D. No violation of the law.

24. In the above example, *Y* would be guilty of

A. Failure to adequately supervise a licensee.
B. Making a misrepresentation through a salesperson.
C. A conflict of interest.
D. No violation of the law.

25. If the lot were not approved for "on site" sewage after the inspection were completed, *Y* would be guilty of

A. A material misrepresentation.
B. Misleading or untruthful advertising.
C. A flagrant course of false promises.
D. No violation of the law.

Answers D., D., D. In 23, *X* would be guilty of no violation of the law even though *X* misrepresented the fact that the lot was approved. The lot was finally approved and the misrepresentation was not "substantial" because *B* was not damaged. Had *B* been damaged and unable to use the lot for the intended purpose, the misrepresentation would have been "substantial" [§604(1)].

In 24, *Y* as the broker for whom *X* worked would be guilty of no misrepresentation and probably not a failure to supervise, unless a flagrant course of conduct by *X* should have put *Y* on notice of *X*'s activities. A broker is not expected to know everything a salesperson may say or do [§604(16)].

In 25, *Y* would not be guilty even though *X* might be guilty of a substantial misrepresentation [§604(16)].

26. *X* a licensed broker is convicted of vehicular homicide. The commission may

A. Automatically suspend *X*'s license.
B. Suspend his license after a hearing at which he is found guilty of vehicular homicide.
C. Suspend his license after a hearing for bad faith.
D. None of the above.

Answer D. *X*'s crime does not involve moral turpitude and, therefore, *X*'s conviction of vehicular homicide may not be grounds for suspension of his license [§604(14)].

27. *X* and *Y* are licensed brokers. *X* has a listing with *S* as seller. *X* offers *Y* a share of the commission if *Y* will find a buyer. *Y* does so and *X* pays a portion of the commission to *Y*. The transaction between *X* and *Y* is not disclosed to *S*. *X* and *Y* together or separately would be guilty of

A. Giving an undisclosed commission in violation of the law.
B. Receiving an undisclosed commission in violation of the law.
C. Conflict of interest.
D. *X* and *Y*, together or individually would not be guilty of a violation.

Answer D. No violation. Nothing prohibits a broker from sharing a commission with another licensed broker. No disclosure to the client is required [§604(10)].

28. What is required if a broker wishes to maintain more than one office in Pennsylvania? The broker
I. Must apply for and obtain an additional license in his name or the name of the associate broker who manages the office.
II. Must have the office registered in his name.

A. I only.
B. II only.
C. Both I and II.
D. Neither I nor II.

Answer B. II only. A branch office must be registered in the name of the broker of record [§601(b)].

29. The commission does not have the power to

A. Suspend a licensee after a hearing.
B. Revoke a license obtained by false representations without a hearing.
C. Levy fines up to $500.
D. None of the above.

Answer B. A licensee is entitled to a hearing before suspension or revocation [§604].

30. Pending receipt of a new license and pocket card changing the affiliation of an associate broker from one broker of record to another, the associate broker

A. Becomes a broker of record.
B. Can continue to engage in brokerage activities.
C. Is under the control of the former employing broker of record.
D. None of the above.

Answer B. The associate broker can continue practice and is under the supervision and control of the new employer [§603].

31. *X*, a licensed broker, arranges the sale of *S*'s property to *B*. A contract between *S* and *B* is executed. *X* refuses to deliver a copy, stating that their respective attorneys must review the contract. The following day *X* provides each with a photocopy of the executed agreement. *X* would be guilty of

A. Failing to provide *S* and *B* with executed original copies of the agreement as prescribed by law.
B. Failing to voluntarily furnish copies of the contract to *S* and *B*.
C. Failing to voluntarily and timely provide copies of the contract to *S* and *B*.
D. No violation.

Answer C. Copies must be delivered voluntarily at the time of execution [§604(9)].

32. *X*, a licensed broker, has a listing contract for the sale of *S*'s house. *X* receives an offer from *B* at the asking price. The offer was contingent upon acceptance by *S* within 72 hours. *X* fails to report the offer to *S* even though *S* was readily available. The offer expires before it was reported to *S*. *X* would be guilty of

A. Conduct which demonstrates incompetency.
B. A substantial misrepresentation.
C. Failing to exercise adequate supervision.
D. No violation of the law.

Answer A. *X* has not exercised reasonable care in failing to report the offer to *S*. This conduct does not meet the standard of care required of brokers and demonstrates incompetency [§604(20)].

33. *X*, a licensed broker may except listings on the understanding that discrimination will be practiced due to

A. Race, color, sex.
B. Marital status.
C. Religious creed, ancestry, national origin.
D. None of the above.

Answer B. There is no prohibition against discrimination based upon marital status [§604(22)].

34. In case of the removal of a broker's office to a new location,

A. Associate brokers become brokers of record.
B. All licensees at that location shall make application to the commission before such removal.
C. The commission will automatically issue a new license with the new office address.
D. None of the above.

Answer D. None of the above. The licensees are permitted to apply up to ten days after removal. The commission will not issue a new license until the new location meets the requirements of a business location and the fee is paid [§601(a)].

35. What must an applicant for a builder-owner salesperson license submit to the commission?
I. A sworn statement by the builder-owner by whom he is employed certifying to such employment.
II. His application so that it is received by the commission within three years of the date upon which the applicant took the examination.

A. I only.
B. II only.
C. Both I and II.
D. Neither I nor II.

Answer C. Both I and II [§551].

36. *B*, a licensed broker, has a listing contract with *S*, the seller of a home, who wants to sell for $50,000. *B*'s wife, *W*, who has retained her maiden name, offers to purchase the property at *S*'s price of $50,000. *S* agrees and sells the property to *W*, who requests that the deed be made with *B* and *W* as grantees. *S* did not know that *W* was *B*'s wife. *B* would be guilty of

   A. Failing to disclose to *S* his interest in the transaction.
   B. Acting for more than one party to a transaction without the knowledge and consent of *S*.
   C. Untruthful advertising.
   D. *B* would be guilty of no violation.

Answer A. *B* must disclose an indirect interest to *S*. The fact that *S* received the full price does not affect *B*'s obligation to disclose his interest [§604(12)].

37. A person required to be affiliated with a licensed broker is a

   A. Rental listing referral agent.
   B. Builder-owner salesperson.
   C. Limited salesperson.
   D. None of the above.

Answer D. None of the above is required to be affiliated with a licensed broker. The limited salesperson may be affiliated with broker but as a minimum is required to be affiliated with a limited broker [§§§551, 561, 541(c)].

38. What must the applicant for a broker's license do before the license is issued?
   I. State in his application the place of business for which such license is desired.
   II. Disclose whether he will be employing an associate broker.

   A. I only.
   B. II only.
   C. Both I and II.
   D. Neither I nor II.

Answer A. I only. A license can only be issued for a specific location [§512].

39. Which of the following activities is not included in the definition of "broker"?
   I. Representing oneself as a real estate consultant or housefinder.
   II. Collecting rental information for the purpose of referring prospective tenants to rental units.

   A. I only.
   B. II only.
   C. Both I and II.
   D. Neither I nor II.

Answer B. II only. A broker's license is not required. However, a rental listing referral agent license is required [§201].

40. By whom may a complaint alleging discrimination by a licensee be investigated?
   I. The Pennsylvania Human Relations Commission.
   II. The Pennsylvania Real Estate Commission.

   A. I only.
   B. II only.
   C. Both I and II.
   D. Neither I nor II.

Answer C. Both I and II. The Pennsylvania Human Relations Commission has up to ninety days to proceed against a licensee before the Real Estate Commission may proceed. But both have authority to investigate [§604(22)].

41. What must a corporation do in order to be licensed as a limited broker?
    I. Designate a limited broker of record.
    II. Qualify for licensure all members intending to engage in the limited brokerage business.

    A. I only.
    B. II only.
    C. Both I and II.
    D. Neither I nor II.

Answer C. Both I and II. The requirements of corporate broker's license are applicable to corporate limited brokers as well [§533].

42. What must be done by a salesperson who receives deposit money incident to a real estate transaction in which he is engaged on behalf of the broker-employer?
    I. Deposit the monies received to the salesperson's custodial or trust account as soon as possible.
    II. Account to all parties to the transactions for all receipts and disbursements.

    A. I only.
    B. II only.
    C. Both I and II.
    D. Neither I nor II.

Answer D. Neither I nor II. The broker employer is responsible for depositing all funds in a custodial or escrow account and accounting to all parties to the transaction for monies received and disbursed [§604(5)].

43. For each transaction involving receipt by the broker of money belonging to another, the broker is required to

    A. Open a separate custodial or escrow account.
    B. Maintain records of the transaction which are subject to inspection by the commission.
    C. Deposit the money within 72 hours.
    D. None of the above.

Answer B. Maintain records of the transaction which are subject to inspection by the commission. The broker need not open a separate account for each transaction; it need only be an account designated as an escrow account separate and apart from the broker's own account. The statute requires the "immediate" deposit of funds and does not specify a time limit [§604(5)].

44. A broker is required to maintain records of the custodial or trust account for at least

    A. Five years following the initiation of the transaction.
    B. Three years following the receipt of monies incident to the transaction.
    C. One year.
    D. None of the above.

Answer D. None of the above. Records must be maintained for three years following *consummation* of the transaction [§604(6)].

45. An application for broker's license shall be made in writing to

A. The Department of State.
B. The Real Estate Commission.
C. The Board of Realtors.
D. None of the above.

Answer A. The application must be submitted to the Department of State [§512].

46. Under what circumstances must a licensee seek prior permission of the commission for engaging in sales activities within Pennsylvania for land located outside Pennsylvania?
I. When the sales are of a "promotional nature."
II. When the sales involve a violation of the licensing law.

A. I only.
B. II only.
C. Both I and II.
D. Neither I nor II.

Answer A. I only. Prior to engaging in sales of a "promotional nature," a licensee must seek the prior approval of the commission [§605].

47. A person seeking money from the Real Estate Recovery Fund must

A. Obtain a judgment in court against the licensee for fraud, misrepresentation, or deceit.
B. Have no other recourse against the licensee, all legal and equitable remedies having been exhausted.
C. Make the application within one year.
D. All of the above.

Answer D. Judgment must be obtained, the aggrieved party must have no other recourse, and the application must be made within one year of the termination of the proceedings against the licensee [§803(b)].

48. If recovery from the Real Estate Recovery Fund is obtained by an aggrieved party against a licensee, the licensee

A. Must repay the money to the fund plus interest.
B. The aggrieved party is barred from further claims of any nature against the licensee.
C. Will automatically have his license suspended.
D. None of the above.

Answer C. The licensee will automatically have his license suspended. Repayment of the funds is a precondition for the reinstatement of a licensee's license. [§803(f)].

49. Before whom must a hearing of the commission take place?
I. The commission or any of its members.
II. Any other person authorized by the commission.

A. I only.
B. II only.
C. Both I and II.
D. Neither I nor II.

Answer C. Both I and II. The commission, its members, its duly authorized representatives, or any other person duly authorized may conduct hearings [§701].

50. What must a broker obtain before he may place a "for sale" sign on the owner's property?

I. A listing.

II. The written consent of the owner or his agent.

A. I only.

B. II only.

C. Both I and II.

D. Neither I nor II.

Answer B. II only. The broker must obtain the permission of the owner or his agent before the broker may place a "for sale" sign on the owner's property [§604(8)].

PART IV

Sample Examination

This sample examination consists of thirty questions dealing with the Pennsylvania Real Estate Licensing Act of 1980. In order to obtain maximum benefit from the sample examination, it is best to do this examination after all of the materials have been studied carefully. It should be used as a final test of the examinee's understanding of both the law and the method for taking the examination.

The examinee may find that the sample examination should be taken under examination-type conditions. Rather than taking the sample examination under ideal conditions in the home or office, it may prove helpful to attempt the examination at another, less comfortable location. For this purpose, the local library may be an alternative. At the library there is enforced silence, but also distractions and unfamiliar surroundings that simulate examination conditions.

The examinee should establish a time limit. One hour should provide enough time to complete the examination. It is best to undertake the task at one sitting and to refrain from checking answers until the examination is completed. Before comparing answers with the key, it is wise to check that all the answers on the answer sheet are filled in and that all extraneous marks on the answer sheet have been erased. If there is time remaining after the examination is taken, answers which are uncertain should be rechecked. In rechecking an answer, be sure to reread the question and each of the answers as if doing it for the first time. This provides another opportunity to view the question and answers. Often a fresh look provides a clue as to the correct answer.

After a final check of the examination and the answer sheet, the answer key should be consulted. All questions which were not answered properly should be checked with the appropriate section of the law. The answer key refers to specific sections of the law.

SAMPLE EXAMINATION

1. The following applicants need not take the salesperson's examination as a requirement for licensure:

   A. Builder-owner salesperson.
   B. Limited salesperson.
   C. Rental listing referral agent.
   D. None of the above.

2. *X,* a properly licensed auctioneer, is contacted by *S*, a seller of residential property to sell *S's* property. In order to be exempt from licensure under the licensing law, what must *X* do?
   I. Perform the services at a bona fide auction.
   II. Be under the direct supervision and control of *S*.

   A. I only.
   B. II only.
   C. Both I and II.
   D. Neither I nor II.

3. A licensee who renews his license but remains inactive must submit to and pass an examination after

   A. One year.
   B. Two years.
   C. Five years.
   D. None of the above.

4. *O* is the owner of a building containing storerooms. *L* is lessee of the building under a ten-year lease with *O*. *L* wishes to sublease part of the building and offers it for sublease in newspaper advertisements and commences negotiations with *S*, a potential sublessee. *S* subsequently subleases the property from *L*. Under these circumstances, *L* would be

   A. Exempt from licensure under the "owner" exemption.
   B. Exempt from licensure because the license law does not apply to subleases.
   C. In violation of the licensing law.
   D. None of the above.

5. When changing employing brokers, an associate broker shall submit to the commission

   A. A new application for licensure.
   B. The written consent of the old employing broker.
   C. His pocket card.
   D. None of the above.

6. Which of the following is a requirement with regard to trust or custodial funds maintained by a broker?
   I. The account must be maintained in a Federal Reserve Bank.
   II. The account must provide for withdrawal of funds without prior notice.

   A. I only.
   B. II only.
   C. Both I and II.
   D. Neither I nor II.

7. A licensee may not make any distinctions in locations of housing for the purposes of discrimination based upon

   A. Economic condition.
   B. Marital status.
   C. National origin.
   D. None of the above.

8. Under what circumstances may a broker's license be suspended or revoked after hearing because of illegal activities of an employee salesperson or associate broker?
   I. If the employing broker had actual knowledge of the activities.
   II. If the employing broker failed to exercise supervision over the activities.

   A. I only.
   B. II only.
   C. Both I and II.
   D. Neither I nor II.

9. What must a claimant against the Real Estate Recovery Fund be required to show before a claim will be paid?
   I. That all reasonable efforts to collect the judgment debt have been exhausted.
   II. That he was defrauded by a licensee.

   A. I only.
   B. II only.
   C. Both I and II.
   D. Neither I nor II.

10. A nonlicensee required by law to possess the reputation requirements of the license law is

    A. Attorney-in-fact.
    B. Builder-owner.
    C. Rental listing referral agent.
    D. None of the above.

11. *X*, acting pursuant to a properly executed recorded power of attorney from *Y*, negotiates the sale of *Y*'s house to *Z*. Under the contract between *X* and *Y*, *X* was to receive a commission for the services performed as *Y*'s attorney-in-fact. *Y* refuses to pay the commission. *X* brings a civil suit against *Y* to recover the unpaid commission. The most likely result of such a law suit would be

    A. Recovery denied because a nonlicensee may not maintain a civil suit to recover a commission for activities limited to licensees.
    B. Recovery granted provided that *X* performed his obligation under the contract.
    C. Recovery denied and *X* is subject to a $500 fine.
    D. None of the above.

12. The Pennsylvania Real Estate Commission has authority to do the following:
    I. Prescribe subjects upon which to examine applicants for licensure.
    II. Approve schools which offer or conduct any course in real estate.

    A. I only
    B. II only.
    C. Both I and II.
    D. Neither I nor II.

13. The authority to arrange for the services of a professional testing service to write and administer the examination is vested in

    A. The Department of State, acting through the Commissioner of Professional and Occupational Affairs.
    B. Real Estate Commission.
    C. Pennsylvania Association of Realtors®.
    D. None of the above.

14. A broker or salesperson licensee in another state is

    A. Exempt from licensure in Pennsylvania.
    B. Permitted to sell out-of-state real estate within Pennsylvania.
    C. Required to maintain a business location within Pennsylvania.
    D. None of the above.

15. Which of the following is true with regard to branch offices?
    I. Each branch office must be under the supervision and control of a broker.
    II. Only the designated broker is directly responsible to the commission for the branch office.

    A. I only.
    B. II only.
    C. Both I and II.
    D. Neither I nor II.

16. Records relating to real estate transactions must be preserved for a period of

    A. Three years following initiation.
    B. Three years following consummation.
    C. Three years following receipt of the earnest money deposit.
    D. None of the above.

17. *X*, a licensed broker, has entered into a listing contract with *S* to negotiate the sale of *S's* farm. *X* is contacted by *B* about the possibility of *X's* rendering services to *B* in assisting to locate a farm property. *X* agrees to assist *B* for a fee; however, no formal written contractual arrangement is entered into by *X* and *B*. *X* shows *B* the farm owned by *S*. What must *X* do under the licensing law?
    I. Obtain the consent in writing of *S*.
    II. Obtain the consent in writing of *B*.

    A. I only.
    B. II only.
    C. Both I and II.
    D. Neither I nor II.

18. *X*, a licensed broker, enters into a listing contract with *Y*, the seller of a recreational property. The listing provides that at the end of the original listing term of 120 days, the listing shall continue for additional periods of 120 days until *Y* gives *X* 30-days' notice prior to the expiration of a 120-day renewal term. Which of the following is true with regard to this situation?
    I. The listing contract violates the licensing law because it may exceed one year.
    II. The listing contract violates the licensing law because it fails to specify a definite termination date that is not subject to prior notice.

    A. I only.
    B. II only.
    C. Both I and II.
    D. Neither I nor II.

19. Which of the following are authorized to conduct hearings under the licensing law?
    I. The commission as a whole or any member thereof.
    II. Any other person, provided that that person is duly authorized by the commission.

    A. I only.
    B. II only.
    C. Both I and II
    D. Neither I nor II.

20. *X*, *Y*, and *Z* are associate brokers employed by *B*. Over a period of two years in twelve separate transactions *X*, *Y*, and *Z* embezzled $25,000 of escrow monies and are convicted in criminal court. At a hearing before the commission on revocation of *B's* license, it is most likely that

    A. *B* will be required to prove that he had no actual knowledge of the activities of *X*, *Y*, and *Z*.
    B. The complaining party will have to prove that *B* had actual knowledge of the activities of *X*, *Y*, and *Z*.
    C. *B* will be found guilty of commingling funds.
    D. None of the above.

21. The commission has the right to assess licensees if the minimum balance of the Real Estate Recovery Fund after January 1, 1982 shall be less than

    A. $100,000.
    B. $500,000.
    C. The amount necessary to cover all anticipated losses.
    D. None of the above.

22. *X*, a licensed broker, is owner of a farm property. *S*, the owner of an adjacent tract, lists his property for sale with *X*'s company. *X*'s wife, *Y*, is interested in purchasing the tract, and *X* tells *S* that *X*'s wife, *Y*, is interested, that *Y* is his wife, and that *X* will be named as a grantee on the deed from *S*. A contract is entered into between *S* and *Y*. Under these circumstances, *X*, would

    A. Be in violation of the license law for not properly disclosing his interest in the manner prescribed by the law.
    B. Not be in violation of the licensing law because he disclosed his interest.
    C. Be in violation for accepting an unauthorized commission because his wife *Y* was the purchaser.
    D. None of the above.

23. *B*, a buyer, gives an earnest money check to *S*, the salesperson, supervised at a branch office by *AB*, an associate broker employed by *X*. Which of the following is required by law?
    I. *S* must promptly pay over the deposit to *AB*.
    II. *AB* must immediately deposit the money in his escrow account.

    A. I only.
    B. II only.
    C. Both I and II.
    D. Neither I nor II.

24. A limited salesperson

    A. May be employed by a broker.
    B. May be employed by an associate broker.
    C. Can do everything a salesperson can do.
    D. None of the above.

25. Which of the following is within the definition of "broker"?
    I. Any person whose main business is that of advertising, promotion, or public relations.
    II. A person who limits his activities solely to the appraisal of commercial leases.

    A. I only.
    B. II only.
    C. Both I and II.
    D. Neither I nor II.

26. The principal individual of a licensed corporation which is engaged in the development and construction of residential real property is the

    A. Builder-owner.
    B. Broker of record.
    C. Designated licensee.
    D. None of the above.

27. The individual whose job it is to handle the day-to-day bookkeeping of the broker's escrow or custodial account is required

    A. To be a salesperson.
    B. To be a licensee.
    C. To meet the reputation requirements of the licensing law.
    D. None of the above.

28. The salesperson applicant must meet which of the following qualifications?
    I. Be 18 years of age.
    II Complete four semester credit hours of 15 hours each.

    A. I only.
    B. II only.
    C. Both I and II
    D. Neither I nor II.

29. Which of the following applicants must meet the qualification for salesperson?
    I. Builder-owner salesperson.
    II. Rental listing referral agent, except that the applicant need not be affiliated with a broker.

    A. I only.
    B. II only.
    C. Both I and II.
    D. Neither I nor II.

30. Which of the following is true?
    I. The duties that apply to brokers also apply to limited brokers.
    II. A limited broker cannot have a branch office.

    A. I only.
    B. II only.
    C. Both I and II.
    D. Neither I nor II.

ANSWERS TO THE SAMPLE EXAMINATION

Question	*Answer*	*Licensing Law Section*
1	B	541
2	A	304
3	D	501(b)
4	A	304
5	C	603
6	B	604(5)(iv), 604(5)(v)
7	C	604(22)(iii)
8	C	604(16), 702
9	A	802(b)
10	B	551(2)
11	B	302, 304
12	C	402, 403
13	A	403
14	D	602(b)
15	C	601(b)
16	B	604(6)
17	C	604(7)
18	B	604(10)
19	C	701(a)
20	A	702
21	D	802
22	A	604(13)
23	D	604(b)(ii)
24	A	201
25	B	201
26	B	201
27	D	201
28	C	521
29	B	551 and 552
30	A	601

Appendices

Rules and Regulations of the State Real Estate Commission

General provisions

1. Definitions.
2. Applicability of general rules.

Real estate brokers

11. Licensing.
12. Individual qualifications for brokers examination.
13. Moral background.
14. Apprenticeship.
15. Education.
16. Sworn statements.
17. Photographs.
18. Fees.
19. Time.

Corporate and partnership requirements for licensure as real estate broker

21. General requirements.
22. Articles of incorporation and relevant records.
23. Sworn statements.
24. Fees.

Limited license as real estate broker

31. General requirements.
32. Examination qualifications.
33. Limited broker's license as corporation or partnership.

Nonresident brokers

41. General requirements.
42. Reciprocity.
43. Filing of consent.
44. Reciprocal office requirements.
45. Return of license.
46. Sanction by licensing authority in reciprocal state.

Place of business of real estate brokers

51. General requirements.
52. Notice.
53. Standards for place of business.
54. Fees.
55. Change of employer.
56. Brokers in employ of another broker.
57. Renewal of license.
58. Business names.

Branch offices

61. General requirements.
62. Termination.
63. Competence of licensee.
64. Supervision and control.
65. Duplicate licenses.
66. Fees.
67. Business names.

Real estate salesmen

71. General requirements.
72. Place of written examinations.
73. Time of written examinations.
74. Processing of application for examination.
75. Permission to reschedule examination.
76. Exemptions from the act.
77. Application for licensure as limited real estate salesman.
78. Issuance of limited license as real estate salesman.

Advertising

81. Misleading advertising.
82. Business name.
83. Additional permissible names.
84. Impermissible advertising.

Basic sales documents

91. Sole or exclusive sales listing contract.
92. Open sales listing contract.
93. Escrow.
94. Statements of estimated cost and return.
95. Agreement of sale.

Ethical considerations and responsibilities

101. Written contracts.
102. Advertising.
103. Validity and veracity of representations.
104. Conflict of interest.
105. Act of a broker in case of corporate or partnership license.
106. Employe supervision by brokers.
107. Violations.
108. Management and appraisal of real estate.
109. Panic selling.
110. Solicitation by brokers.

GENERAL PROVISIONS

1. Definitions.

The following words and terms, when used in this Chapter, shall have the following meanings, unless the context clearly indicates otherwise.

Act — The Real Estate Brokers License Act of one thousand nine hundred and twenty-nine (63 P.S. §§ 431–438).

Commission — The State Real Estate Commission.

Hardship case — Any individual who has satisfactorily completed two of the three years apprenticeship requirement but who does not have either home or business address within a radius of 60 miles of an approved school with classroom instruction; or who cannot attend such a school because of physical disability.

Semester credit — A period of 15 standard hours of instruction.

Standard hour of instruction — A period of fifty minutes. However, for qualification under the requirements of this Chapter, no one course shall be credited with more than three semester credits and no more than two courses in the same subject shall be credited toward the professional educational requirements.

2. Applicability of general rules.

Pursuant to 1 Pa. Code § 31.1 (relating to scope of part), the General Rules of Administrative Practice and Procedure, 1 Pa. Code Part II, are applicable to the activities of and proceedings before the Commission.

11. Licensing.

To secure a license as a real estate broker, a person, properly qualified as provided in 12 of this Title (relating to individual qualifications for brokers' examination), shall submit a written application for licensure to the Commission and have a place of business approved by the Commission as meeting the standards set forth in 51–58 of this Title (relating to place of business of real estate brokers).

12. Individual qualifications for brokers' examination.

Applicants for the brokers' examination shall meet the following qualifications:

(1) Be at least 21 years of age.

(2) Have a background of good moral behavior. Reference should also be made to 13 of this Title (relating to moral background).

(3) Have served a full time apprenticeship in active practice as a duly licensed real estate salesman of not less than three years in the employ of a duly licensed real estate broker or brokers.

(4) Have fulfilled the professional educational requirements prescribed in 141–148 of this Title (relating to real estate education) in a school approved by the commission.

13. Moral background.

(a) Each applicant shall submit recommendations for licensure containing a declaration as to his honesty, truthfulness and good reputation by at least two persons, not related to the applicant, who are citizens and owners of real estate in the county where the applicant resides or has his place of business; a similar recommendation shall be given by one real estate broker licensed in this Commonwealth. If the applicant has resided for less than one year in the county from which application is made, similar recommendations shall also be submitted by two persons who are citizens and real property owners in the county where the applicant previously resided.

(b) Each applicant shall provide a complete consecutive record of his employment for the five year period immediately preceding the application and, in addition, shall state whether or not he has been arrested or convicted of any crime, minor traffic offenses excepted. If answer is yes, complete details of the incident including disposition shall be given.

14. Apprenticeship.

(a) An apprenticeship in active practice for three years, requires that the applicant shall have been a duly licensed salesman of a duly licensed broker, or brokers, and engaged on a full time basis on behalf of such broker or brokers for three years and shall have acquired substantial experience in all aspects of the real estate business.

(b) To satisfy the requirements of this section the applicant shall see that the apprenticeship includes practice and experience in all phases of the real estate business.

(c) Each applicant for licensure as a real estate broker shall submit a complete resume of activities while serving as an apprentice, and a sworn statement by his employing brokers, giving a detailed account of the real estate activities in which the applicant engaged as a real estate salesman while in their employ. The commission will give consideration to satisfactory evidence of diversified activities in sales, rentals, listings and mortgages as outlined in the complete resume and sworn statement of employing brokers.

15. Education.

To establish satisfactory completion of the educational requirements prescribed in 141–148 of this Title (relating to real estate education), an applicant shall present with his application for licensure examination a formal transcript from the school certifying satisfactory completion of the required courses.

16. Sworn statements.

(a) Applications, statements and papers required to be filed by or on behalf of an applicant for a broker's license under the act and this Chapter shall be under oath and shall be subject to such investigation as the Commission may deem necessary to determine their accuracy and truthfulness.

(b) Statements submitted by an individual in connection with his application shall be under oath; this includes the statements of his character references. Failure on the part of either the applicant or any of his broker sponsors to give accurate and truthful information in the application or accompanying statements constitutes a ground for the denial of the application or the suspension or revocation of the license of the offending party.

17. Photographs.

Each application for a license submitted by an individual shall be accompanied by two unmounted photographs of the applicant, which shall be 1½ by 1½ inches, on thin paper, white background, front view in street clothes, without hat, and should be signed by the applicant in ink on the back. Snapshots, group pictures, proofs of quick finished pictures are not acceptable.

18. Fees.

Each application shall be accompanied by a certified check or money order in the sum of $25.00 for initial examination and $10.00 for re-examination, payable to the Commonwealth of Pennsylvania—R.E.

19. Time.

If a person has been qualified and has been approved to take the real estate broker's examination, and has not successfully completed the examination within one year thereafter, he shall submit a new application meeting the current requirements, if he desires to take the broker's examination again.

CORPORATE AND PARTNERSHIP REQUIREMENTS FOR LICENSURE AS REAL ESTATE BROKER

21. General requirements.

(a) A partnership, association or corporation may be licensed as a real estate broker, if all members of any such partnership or association or all officers of any such corporation who intend to engage in or actually engage in the real estate business themselves are duly licensed as real estate brokers.

(b) There shall be one corporate officer designated in the application for the corporate broker's license who shall be a licensed real estate broker or an applicant who has successfully completed his examination for such license, and the proposed chief executive officer of the corporation who is in charge of real estate transactions.

(c) Any other officer of the corporation, as defined in subsection (a) of this section, except the applicant named under subsection (b) of this section, who intends to engage in the real estate business of the corporation shall have an individual broker's license giving his place of business as that of a corporation, which license shall not issue unless the officer is a licensed broker or applicant who meets all the requirements for licensure and who has successfully completed his examination for such license.

(d) Section 7 of the act (63 P.S. § 437) provides that one corporate officer shall be designated as the individual possessing the authority to transact the business of the corporation under the corporate broker's license. It follows from the nature of that authority that the officer named as possessing it shall also be the chief executive officer of the corporation in charge of real estate transactions. The possession of such authority also places the person involved squarely within the provisions of the act which requires that any officer intending to engage in the real estate business of a corporation shall be licensed as a real estate broker. In order to be a broker, however, section 9 of the act (63 P.S. § 439) requires that any person, including a corporation officer, have and maintain a definite place of business.

22. Articles of incorporations and relevant records.

The corporate applicant shall make available, upon request, its articles of incorporation, stock register, stock certificates and other relevant records and data.

23. Sworn statements.

Each partnership member and each corporation officer and employer shall submit under oath the following:

(1) An account of his background, including a complete consecutive record of his employment for the five year period immediately preceding the application.

(2) A statement as to whether or not he has ever been arrested for any crime, with the exception of minor traffic offenses. If answer is "yes," applicant shall give complete details of the incident.

24. Fees.

Each application for a corporate real estate broker's license shall be accompanied by a certified check or money order, in the sum of $25.00 payable to the Commonwealth of Pennsylvania—R.E.

LIMITED LICENSE AS REAL ESTATE BROKER

31. General requirements.

(a) A limited real estate broker's license may be issued to any person, partnership, association or corporation desiring to engage in or carry on the business of a real estate broker exclusively within the limited field or branch of such business which applies to cemetery lots, plots and mausoleum spaces or openings.

(b) To secure a limited license as a real estate broker, a written application shall be submitted to the Commission and a written examination shall be successfully completed.

32. Examination qualifications.

To qualify as a candidate for examination for a limited license as a real estate broker, the applicant shall meet the same requirements as those in connection with licensure as a real estate broker, including the education requirements as outlined in 141—148 of this Title (relating to real estate education), except that his apprenticeship as a salesman may be limited to the branch of real estate brokerage for which he seeks a limited broker's license. Each application for a limited license shall be accompanied by two unmounted photographs which shall meet the standards required for licensure as a real estate broker as set forth in 17 of this Title (relating to photographs) and shall be accompanied by a certified check or money order in the sum of $25.00 for initial examination and $10.00 for re-examination, payable to the Commonwealth of Pennsylvania—R.E.

33. Limited broker's license as corporation or partnership.

(a) *Licensed members.* There shall be one corporate officer designated in the application for the limited broker's license who shall be a duly licensed real estate broker or limited broker, or an applicant who has successfully completed his examination for such license. The application shall clearly show the name and addresses of all corporate officers with their titles and indicate whether they will be active or inactive in the selling of cemetery lots, plots, mausoleum spaces in connection with the corporation.

(b) *Nonlicensed members.* Each nonlicensed member of the partnership and each nonlicensed corporate officer shall state under oath, whether he is a citizen of the United States; an account of his background including a complete consecutive record of his employment for the five year period immediately preceding the application; and whether or not he has ever been arrested for any crime, with the exception of minor traffic offenses. If answer to arrest is "yes," applicant shall give complete details including disposition.

NONRESIDENT BROKERS

41. General requirements.

(a) Persons who are not residents of this Commonwealth, shall be licensed in this Commonwealth as real estate brokers or real estate salesmen if they are dealing in real estate, regardless of whether such real estate is located in this Commonwealth, if any part of the transaction affecting real estate is to take place in this Commonwealth, and if performing such part of the transaction constitutes the business of real estate broker or real estate salesman as those terms are defined in the Act.

(b) A non-resident of this Commonwealth may be licensed as a real estate broker or real estate salesman if in his application for licensure he submits, in lieu of the recommendations and statements required of resident applicants, a certification from the licensing authority of the state of his domicile which shall indicate length of time applicant held a salesman's license and broker's license, and which shall state clearly if the license was secured by passing a required written examination.

(c) The provisions of this section shall apply only to licensed real estate brokers and real estate salesmen of those states whose laws and examinations are similar to these of this Commonwealth, and whose laws extend similar recognition and courtesies to licensed real estate brokers and real estate salesmen of this Commonwealth.

42. Reciprocity.

Applicants applying for a license on the basis of reciprocity shall:

(1) be a non-resident of this Commonwealth,
(2) have met this Commonwealth's minimum education requirements for licensure,

(3) have obtained licensure in the state of his domicile by passing a written examination and
(4) submit a certification by the licensing authority of the state of domicile of the following:
  (i) license number of current license and date issued,
  (ii) statement as to the length of time licensee has been licensed as a real estate broker or salesman or both and whether he holds a valid renewal for the current year,
  (iii) office address of applicant, if broker, name and address of employing broker, if an associate broker or salesperson,
  (iv) statement showing complaint record, if charges have been made and are pending, or if formal action has been taken, an explanation of such charges and such action, and
  (v) statement showing that applicant received licensure by successfully passing a written examination.

43. Filing of consent.

The application for a real estate broker or salesman license shall be accompanied by a written consent that suits or actions in law or in equity arising out of the licensee's real estate activities in this Commonwealth, may be commenced against such applicant in the proper court of any county of this Commonwealth in which a cause of action may arise, by service of process upon the Secretary of the Commonwealth and upon the Chairman of the Commission.

44. Reciprocal office requirements.

(a) A reciprocal broker applicant shall maintain an office in either the state of his domicile or in this Commonwealth. No office is required in this Commonwealth if an office is maintained in the state of domicile.

(b) An office maintained in this Commonwealth by a reciprocally licensed broker shall meet the same standards and requirements imposed upon other real estate offices operating in this Commonwealth.

(c) If the broker who has secured a Pennsylvania license through reciprocity elects to open an office or offices in this Commonwealth, all real estate activity conducted in this Commonwealth shall be conducted through those offices.

45. Return of license.

(a) If a non-resident broker who obtained a license through reciprocity ceases to comply with the office requirement set forth in 44(a) of this Title (relating to reciprocal office requirements) he shall return his Pennsylvania broker license to the Commission for cancellation.

(b) Any real estate salesman whose employing broker's license has been revoked or cancelled in this Commonwealth shall return his Pennsylvania license to the Commission for escrowing until such time as said real estate salesman shall be reemployed by a qualified broker.

46. Sanction by licensing authority in reciprocal state.

A licensee who has obtained licensure in this Commonwealth on the basis of reciprocity, shall within 30 days of receiving notice, notify the Commission of any sanction imposed upon him by the licensing authority of his domicile state or by the licensing authority of a state in which he holds a real estate license.

PLACE OF BUSINESS OF REAL ESTATE BROKERS

51. General requirements.

Every person, partnership, association or corporation licensed as a real estate broker, except a nonresident broker licensed under the provisions of 41–45 of this Title (relating to nonresident brokers) and section 7(e) of the act (63 P.S. § 437(e)) but including any limited broker, shall have and maintain a definite place of business within this Commonwealth.

52. Notice.

(a) A broker's license will not be issued until the applicant has notified the Commission of his proposed place of business and approval of this place of business has been given.

(b) Place of business, within the meaning of subsection (a) of this section, includes the place of employment when the applicant is applying for an associate-broker's status under 56 of this Title (relating to broker in employ of another broker).

53. Standards for place of business.

A place of business will be approved by the Commission in accordance with the following standards:

(1) If located in a commercial building or a private dwelling, it shall have at least one room to be used by the broker exclusively for the transaction of his real estate and allied business.

(2) If the office is in a private dwelling, the entrance to such place shall be separate and apart from the entrance to any room or rooms used for purposes other than a real estate and allied business, and no portion of the office shall be used to obtain access to other rooms in such dwelling.

(3) A real estate office devoted to the transaction of real estate business shall include as a minimum the following:

- (i) One standard size desk.
- (ii) Four chairs.
- (iii) One four drawer filing cabinet.
- (iv) Waiting area with seating capacity for at least two persons.
- (v) Place arranged to permit business to be conducted in a private and confidential manner.
- (vi) One additional desk for each two salesmen or associate brokers employed.

54. Fees.

The approved place of business shall be designated in the license of the broker and a licensee may not transact business from any other place except from branch offices established in accordance with 61–67 of this Title (relating to branch offices), or from a new business location if notice in writing of such change, together with a fee of $5.00 shall be sent to the Commission within ten days of such change.

55. Change of employer.

Any real estate broker who enters the employ of another broker shall discontinue his own place of business and his place of business shall be that of his employer.

56. Brokers in employ of another broker.

A broker in the employ of another broker shall observe the following:

(1) He shall return his broker's license to the office of the Commission and shall receive a license bearing the classification "associate broker."

(2) In his capacity as an associate broker, he shall be entitled to do all things which a broker may do except the following:

- (i) Employ salesmen or other brokers or associate brokers.
- (ii) Engage in the real estate business in his own name or in his own place of business.

57. Renewal of license.

Any person who has held a license as a real estate broker or associate broker may renew his license without examination at any time within seven years of the date the license became inactive if such person provides satisfactory proof that he has and maintains a place of business which meets the minimum standards established by the Commission. This section does not apply where the broker's license was surrendered while under investigation or suspended or revoked for a violation of the act or the provisions of this Chapter.

58. Business names.

(a) *Designation.* The name under which such broker conducts his business shall be the name designated in his license together with the words "real estate," "realty" or, if applicable, "realtor" or "realtist."

(b) *Display.* Such business name shall appear prominently on the outside of the place of business.

(c) *Determination.* Whether the entire name of the licensee shall be used as the business name in any designation or advertisement will depend on the following considerations:

(1) In the case of a single proprietor or practitioner, the entire name shall be used except that the last name may be given greater printed emphasis.

(2) In the case of a joint or partnership business, it is permissible to use only the last names of the licensees in the business name, if the full names of such licensees also appear in a reasonable proximity to such business name in accordance with the standards set forth in 83 of this Title (relating to additional permissible names).

BRANCH OFFICES

61. General requirements.

Every branch office shall be maintained and operated only by the licensed broker to whom the license for such office is issued. A branch office shall not be conducted, maintained and operated under an arrangement whereby the purpose, intent or effect shall permit a licensed salesman, associate broker or other employe to carry on the business for his sole benefit.

62. Termination.

A branch office license shall terminate with the discontinuance, revocation or suspension, for whatever reason, of the original license of the broker, and the Commission may cancel any branch office license or revoke or suspend the broker's original license for any violation of this Chapter.

63. Competence of licensee.

A branch office license shall not be issued to an original broker licensee unless it appears to the satisfaction of the Commission that with the additional branch office, such broker will not be rendered incapable of exercising proper service to his principals including the exercising of a reasonable degree of supervision over his salesmen's or associate broker's activities at his different places of business.

64. Supervision and control.

Every branch office shall be under the supervision and control of the broker to whom the license is issued.

65. Duplicate licenses.

A broker shall not open an office in addition to that specified in his license unless he first obtains a duplicate license; such duplicate license shall be identical to the original license except that it shall contain, in addition, the address of the branch office.

66. Fees.

For purposes of obtaining branch office license approval, each branch office license will be considered a separate license which may be obtained by filing the required application and fee of $10.

67. Business names.

A branch office license shall not be issued under any other name than the name under which the broker is licensed to conduct business at his main office. Reference should also be made to 58 of this Title (relating to business names).

REAL ESTATE SALESMEN

71. General requirements.

(a) To secure a license as a real estate salesman, an individual shall submit an appropriate written application to the Commission and satisfactorily complete a written examination.

(b) A candidate for such licensing examination must be at least 18 years of age and shall submit an application for examination designating the name and license number of the real estate broker with whom he shall be associated who will certify that the applicant is honest, truthful and of good repute, and recommend that the applicant be permitted to sit for the examination.

(c) Applications, statements and papers to be filed by or on behalf of an applicant for licensure under the act and this Chapter shall be under oath and shall be subject to such investigation as the Commission may require to determine their accuracy and truthfulness.

72. Place of written examinations.

Examinations are held in the cities of Erie, Harrisburg, Philadelphia, Pittsburgh, and Wilkes-Barre, and such other locations in this Commonwealth as the Commission may direct.

73. Time of written examinations.

Examinations for all forms of real estate licensure are held on the second Saturday of February, May, August and November in the cities set forth in §35.72 of this Title (relating to place of written examinations). In addition, examinations for salesmen's and limited broker's licensure, and builder-owner salesman's certification may be held in Harrisburg on the second Saturday of other months and also may be held at other times and locations as the Commission shall direct.

74. Processing of application for examination.

(a) The properly completed application shall be filed with the office of the Commission. The Commission will schedule applicants for the next available examination on a first come first served basis. If the Commission determines to hold salesman, limited broker and builder-owner salesman examinations on a monthly basis, applicants whose applications were received during the first ten days of a month will be scheduled for the examination on the second Saturday of the following month. The Commission reserves the right to change the examination date to avoid holidays such as Easter Sunday and Veterans Day. Prior announcement will be made of a change in date of any examination.

(b) Applicants who apply for an examination and fail to timely advise the Commission of their inability to attend shall forfeit their examination fee. Notification of non-attendance must be received in writing by the Commission prior to the twentieth of the month preceding the scheduled examination. If timely notice of non-attendance is received, the examination fee will not be returned, however, the applicant will be scheduled for another examination without additional charge.

(c) Broker applicants must file their applications for examination in the Commission Office not later than the 15th day of the month preceding the February, May, August, or November examinations. Both salesperson and broker applicants may only file one application at a time.

(d) Persons who fail an examination may not refile an application until they are officially notified of failure. Examination results should be received within 30 days after the examination. A copy of the official fail notice must be attached to the application for re-examination. Persons who have taken the examination and who have not received their examination results within thirty days should so advise the Commission.

75. Permission to reschedule examination.

An applicant, who, because of religious scruples, cannot take the examination on Saturday, shall in his application, request permission to be given the examination on another day. Bona fide requests will be granted and the examination will generally be given on the Sunday following the regularly scheduled Saturday examination.

76. Exemptions from the act.

A real estate broker's or salesman's license is not required of any person, firm, association, partnership or corporation if the following characteristics are present:

(1) A party as owner of property transacts real estate business with respect to such property. In the case of a partnership or corporation, such exemption shall only extend to all of its partners or officers, respectively, but to no other partnership or corporation personnel or employe.

(2) A party holds in good faith a duly executed letter of attorney from the actual owner of any real estate, authorizing the sale, conveyance or leasing of such real estate for and in the name of such owner or the negotiating of any loan therefor. A person does not hold a letter or power of attorney in good faith if, by reason of his otherwise having been engaged in the business of real estate, his proposed activity involving the real estate of his principal cannot be deemed to be an isolated transaction. In addition, the letter of attorney is not effective unless it is recorded in the office of the Recorder of Deeds prior to initiating, under its authority, any transactions or activities within the scope of practice of a licensed broker set forth in section 2 of the act (63 P.S. § 432).

(3) A party is an attorney at law, and he does not hold himself out as a real estate broker.

(4) A party is a district justice.

(5) A party is a receiver, trustee in bankruptcy, administrator or executor or any other person or corporation acting under the appointment or order of any court, or as trustee under the authority of a will or deed of trust where only the transactions pertaining thereto are involved.

(6) A party is the duly elected executive officer of any banking institution or trust company operating under the banking laws of this Commonwealth where only real estate of the banking institution or trust company is involved, but to no other personnel or employee.

77. Application for licensure as limited real estate salesman.

(a) Each applicant shall submit a statement from his prospective broker employer attesting to his honesty, truthfulness, and good reputation and recommending his licensure as a salesman.

(b) Each applicant shall provide a complete consecutive record of his employment for the five year period immediately preceding the application.

(c) Each applicant shall attach to his application photographs meeting standards as set forth in 16 of this Title (relating to sworn statements) and a certified check or money order in the sum of $5.00, payable to the Commonwealth of Pennsylvania—R.E.

78. Issuance of limited license as real estate salesman.

(a) A limited real estate salesman's license may be issued to any person employed by any limited licensed real estate broker to assist him within the limited field or branch of the brokerage business involving cemetery lots, plots and mausoleum spaces or openings.

(b) A limited salesman's license shall clearly state on its face the field or branch to which such license is applicable. The holder of any such limited license shall not engage in or carry on the business or act in the capacity of a real estate salesman except in such specified limited field.

ADVERTISING

81. Misleading advertising.

Advertising is misleading when, taken as a whole, there is a distinct possibility that it will deceive the ordinary real estate purchaser, seller, landlord, or tenant or other person whom it is intended to influence.

82. Business name.

The business name of a broker, as defined in 58 of this Title (relating to business names), shall be displayed in any real estate advertisement by the broker or his agents whether by newspaper, magazine, circular or other publication or advertising media.

83. Additional permissible names.

In addition to the business name, advertising may contain the name of the real estate broker, or the names of any associate brokers or duly licensed salesmen in his employ, if such names are displayed with sufficiently less prominence so as to leave the clear impression of the connection of the persons named with a specific real estate firm and are accompanied by language showing the status of the persons so named. If the telephone number of the salesmen is included in the newspaper advertisement, the telephone number of the broker shall also be included in a more prominent nature.

84. Impermissible advertising.

(a) A real estate salesman shall not advertise under his own name or place his name on "for rent" or "for sale" signs.

(b) The unauthorized use by a broker of any trade-marked or copyrighted term limited in use to the members of certain real estate organizations or groups is deemed to be misleading advertising within the meaning of the act.

BASIC SALES DOCUMENTS

91. Sole or exclusive sales listing contract.

(a) A sole or exclusive sales listing contract may comprise either exclusive agency of the broker or an exclusive right to sell. No broker shall use a document providing for an exclusive right to sell unless it carries the statement on its face in bold type to the effect that "the broker earns his commission on the sale, by whomsoever made, including the owner."

(b) Every exclusive sales listing contract, regardless of type, shall contain the following terms:

(1) Asking price.
(2) Commission expected on such price.
(3) Terms of payment of the sale price.
(4) Duration of the contract.

(c) An exclusive sales contract shall not contain any of the following provisions:

(1) A period of duration exceeding one year.
(2) An automatic renewal clause.
(3) A cancellation notice to terminate the contract at the end of the term set forth in the contract.
(4) Power by the broker to execute a signed agreement of sale for the owner.
(5) An option by the broker to purchase the property covered by the listing contract.
(6) Authority to the broker in the event of sale to confess judgment against the owner for the commission.

(d) The following exclusive listing contract attached hereto as Exhibit A and made a part of this regulation is exemplary of the standards of this section and 93 if this Title (relating to escrow).

Exhibit A

EXCLUSIVE LISTING CONTRACT

The undersigned hereby appoints____________as the sole and exclusive agent for, and grants said agent the exclusive right to sell, premised located at_______for the sale price of $______.

It is hereby agreed that this contract be in force for______ months from the date hereof and shall then terminate unless extended in writing by the parties hereto.

If said property shall be sold or exchanged during the term of this contract, by this AGENT or by the OWNER, or by any OTHER PERSON, the undersigned agrees to pay the agent a commission of_____% of the gross sale price.

After the termination of this agreement or any extension thereof, the agent's authority shall continue as to negotiations pending at time of such termination, and if subsequent to such termination the property is sold or exchanged to any legal person with whom the agent or owner or other broker shall have negotiated during the term of this contract, the said commission is to be paid to the agent by owner.

The undersigned represents that he has the legal right to sell the property, and has received an exact copy of this agreement.

The agent is hereby authorized to place a "For Sale" sign upon said property which shall be the only such sign permitted to be displayed thereon during the term of this contract.

Owner is hereby notified and understands that all payments on account of this transaction shall be retained in escrow for the benefit of the parties of this transaction in accordance with the Real Estate Licensing Law of the Commonwealth of Pennsylvania.

IN WITNESS WHEREOF, the undersigned has hereunto set his hand and seal this_______day of________19____ .

Accepted:
Agent____________________________ ____________________________
(SEAL) Owner

Address____________________________ ____________________________
(SEAL) Owner

Phone ____________________________ Phone ____________________________

---

92. Open sales listing contract.

Any broker taking an open sales listing contract for sale of real estate shall give to the party involved a written memorandum stating all terms of such listing.

93. Escrow.

Regardless of the form of the listing, each broker for a seller principal shall conclude an agreement or agreements with such principal which meets the requirements of 121 of this Title (relating to escrow requirements) and, if applicable, those of 126 of this Title (relating to multiple listing agreements).

94. Statements of estimated cost and return.

(a) Before an agreement of sale is entered into by the parties, the broker for the seller principal or brokers, if the buyer is also represented, shall observe the following requirements:

(1) Provide written statements of estimated cost and return to the buyer and seller, as the case may be, which includes an itemization for the party responsible for paying them, of the amount of the following charges:
- (i) Commission of the broker.
- (ii) Settlement expenses.
- (iii) Taxes, water bills and other such charges.
- (iv) Financing costs, charges, and any other expense for which there is a reasonable possibility that the party may be liable, or be responsible for as a result of the transaction.
- (v) The amount of the mortgage payments which the purchaser shall pay as a result of this transaction.

(2) Insure that such statements and the estimates which they contain are as accurate as is to be expected of persons having special knowledge and experience in this field.

(b) The following statement of estimated costs to buyer at settlement attached hereto as Exhibit B and made a part of this regulation is exemplary of the requirements of this section.

(c) The following statement of estimated return to seller at settlement attached hereto as Exhibit C and made a part of this regulation is exemplary of the requirements of this section.

95. Agreement of sale.

(a) Any broker involved in the sale of interest in real estate shall voluntarily furnish a copy of the agreement of sale to the buyer and seller. Such agreement shall not be deemed to have been given unless the following provisions appear:

(1) Date of agreement.

(2) Names of parties.

(3) Description of real estate and interest therein to be conveyed.

(4) Consideration for such conveyance.

(5) Date for conveyance and payment. In the case of sales agreements covering homes under construction, this term shall make the contract conditioned upon the following:
- (i) Construction starting by fixed date.
- (ii) Completion by fixed date.

(6) In the case of properties located in cities of the first and second class, a statement showing the zoning classification involved and whether the present use of property is in compliance with or in violation of zoning laws or ordinances, as required by the act of July 27, 1955, P.L. 288, as amended (21 P.S. §611).

(b) No agreement of sale, as defined by the act and this Chapter shall contain the following provisions unless printed in bold face type or, if written or typed, underscored:

(1) Provision relieving a builder or seller from the responsibility for any defects involving the premises or requiring the purchaser to execute releases to that effect at the time of settlement or any provision of similar import.

Exhibit B
STATEMENT OF ESTIMATED COSTS TO BUYER AT SETTLEMENT

Estimated Settlement Date ______________________

Property ______________________

Broker ______________________

Purchase Price	______		
Payment on Account	______		
Balance at Settlement		______	
Estimated Closing Expenses			
Title Search and Insurance	______		
Conveyancing or Preparation of Papers Charge	______		
Recording Fees			
Deed	______		
Mortgage	______	______	
Mortgagee's Charges			
Appraisal Fee	______		
Credit Report	______		
Origination and Placement Fees	______		
Mortgage Service Charge	______		
Fire Insurance ($______ for______ years)			
Miscellaneous Charges			______
Local Realty Transfer Tax	(______%)	______	
Notary Fees	______		
Other Charges	______	______	
Total Closing Expenses			______
Costs for Rebates and Advances			
Rebates to Seller			
Insurance	______		
Annual Taxes and Water-Sewer Rents	______	______	______
Advances by Buyer			
Insurance	______		
Taxes (Escrow)	______	______	
Total Costs for Rebates and Advances			______
Total Estimated Costs at Settlement			______
Estimated Monthly Payments			______
First Lien $______ ______years at ______%			
Interest and Principal		______	
Monthly FHA Mortgage		______	
Insurance Premium		______	
Real Estate Taxes	$______ ÷ 12	$______	
Fire Insurance	$______ ÷ 12	$______	
Water-Sewer Rents	$______ ÷ 12	$______	
Total Estimated Monthly Payments			$______

I/we hereby agree that I/we have read and received a copy of the estimated settlement costs and estimated monthly carrying charges prior to the signing of an agreement of sale to purchase the property noted above.

I/we further understand that the above costs are estimated and based on the best information available at this date and that they are subject to changes, particularly in the case of the escrow charges such as taxes, water and sewage, rent and insurance.

WITNESS:

______________________ ______________________(SEAL)
Buyer

______________________ ______________________(SEAL)
Buyer

Exhibit C

STATEMENT OF ESTIMATED RETURN TO SELLER AT SETTLEMENT

Estimated Settlement Date ____________________

Property ____________________

Broker ____________________

Purchase Price	________	________
Payment on Account	________	
Balance		________
Estimated Closing Expenses		
Penna. Realty Transfer Tax (________ %)	________	
Federal Documentary Stamps	________	
Notary Fee	________	
Mortgage Discount	________	
Unpaid Annual Taxes	________	
Unpaid Water-Sewer Rents	________	
Broker's Commission	________	
Total Expenses		________
Estimated Closing Credits		
Insurance Refund	________	
Tax Refund	________	
Estimated Net Charges		________
Estimated Net Proceeds		________

WITNESS:

________________ ________________
Seller

________________ ________________
Seller

(2) Provision which reserves to builder the right to change or depart from the nature of the house as it was originally described in the contract in terms of the sample house or otherwise.

(c) If an agreement of sale is conditioned upon the ability of the buyer to obtain mortgage financing, such agreement shall indicate the following:

(1) Type and principal amount of mortgage.
(2) Maximum interest rate and minimum term.
(3) Terminal date for obtaining the mortgage.
(4) Nature and extent of assistance to be rendered buyer by a broker and where such assistance is rendered, the dual obligation of the broker to advise buyer in writing when mortgage commitment is obtained and to give buyer, at that time, no less than ten days advance notice of date of settlement.

ETHICAL CONSIDERATIONS AND RESPONSIBILITIES

101. Written contracts.

(a) Each broker acting in any representative capacity in connection with real estate transaction shall ensure that all contracts, commitments and agreements regarding the real estate transaction of which he has or should have knowledge are in writing.

(b) No broker shall be a party to any material false or inaccurate statements in such instruments.

(c) Copies of such instruments shall be retained by the broker concerned for a period of three years.

102. Advertising.

No broker shall advertise or offer to sell or lease property without the authority of the owner or agent of the owner.

103. Validity and veracity of representations.

No broker shall make representations to give assurances or advice concerning any aspect of a real estate transaction which he knows or should know to be incorrect, inaccurate or improbable.

104. Conflict of interest.

(a) No broker shall assume or purport to represent more than one party to a real estate transaction unless all parties expressly agree in writing to such multiple representation.

(b) No broker shall acquire an interest in or buy for himself, his firm or any members thereof or for a corporation in which he has any interest, property listed with him or his firm unless the broker first discloses in writing his interest and position to the listing owners.

(c) No broker acting as agent in the management of property shall accept any commission, rebate, or profit on expenditures made for an owner without knowledge and written consent of the owner.

(d) No broker engaged in the business of financing the purchase of real or personal property or of lending money on the security of real or personal property may require as a condition precedent to such activities the negotiation by the buyer through a particular insurance company of a policy of insurance or the renewal of such insurance covering the property or the person involved, with the exception of a group creditor policy.

105. Act of a broker in case of corporate or partnership license.

Acts that are required to be done by a broker shall, in the case of a corporate or partnership license, be done by the officer or partner designated in the license of such corporation or partnership and, if applicable, the officer specifically charged with performing such act.

106. Employe supervision by brokers.

(a) Any broker having authority to conduct a place of business shall provide a reasonable degree of supervision and control over his associate brokers, licensed salesmen and office staff. In the case of a corporate or partnership licensee, where authority to conduct the business rests with the officer or partner broker designated in the license of such corporation or partnership, such broker shall, in the same manner, also supervise his fellow officers or partners, as applicable.

(b) A broker shall be responsible for violations of the act or this Chapter by his associate brokers, salesmen or employes in accordance with section 14 of the act (63 P.S. §444). A course of dealing shown to have been followed by such associate brokers, salesmen or employes shall constitute *prima facie* evidence of such knowledge upon the part of his employer.

107. Violations.

Acts and conduct which constitute violations of the act and this Chapter, when committed by brokers, are, to the extent applicable, violations of the act and this Chapter when committed by an associate broker or salesman in the employ of the broker.

108. Management and appraisal of real estate.

(a) No salesman shall manage or appraise real estate.

(b) Inasmuch as there is a lack of authority of any licensed salesman to manage or appraise real estate, the proper carrying out of such activities by a firm shall be the personal responsibility of the licensed broker.

109. Panic selling.

(a) Panic selling as used in this section shall mean frequent efforts to sell residential real estate in a particular neighborhood as a result of fear of a decline in real estate values, when the fear is not based on facts relating to the intrinsic value of the real estate itself.

(b) Attempts by real estate brokers or salesmen to bring about panic selling, in order to profit from it, shall constitute incompetency and bad faith within the meaning of the act.

(c) Proof of systematic solicitation of listings of sales shall be sufficient, but not conclusive evidence of an attempt to bring about panic selling.

110. Solicitation by brokers.

A real estate broker, whether or not acting on behalf of a buyer principal, or for no principal, shall not solicit by personal contact, advertising, phone or mail, the sale of other disposition of real estate property with such frequency as to amount to clear harassment of the owner or other persons controlling the sale or disposition of such property.

ESCROW REQUIREMENTS

121. Nature of escrow duty.

(a) *Nonwaivable.* The duty of a real estate broker to escrow funds which he receives is not waived or altered in any manner by any agreement, whether between the parties to a real estate transaction or with the broker or brokers concerned.

(b) *Essential escrow provisions of selling brokerage agreements.* Every real estate broker shall include, in every agreement, whether oral or written, governing the agency relationship between a real estate broker licensed under the act and his seller principal the understanding that all payments of money, paid on account of the real estate transaction contemplated by the agreement, regardless of the form that payment is made, and if by instruments, regardless of the person designated as payee, shall be retained by the broker in an escrow or trust account for the benefit of the parties to the transaction.

(c) *Escrow of security deposits received by brokers when renting property or apartments.* Every broker, when acting as rental agent for property, shall state in the lease or his agency agreement, that the broker will hold the security deposit during the term designated in the lease. At termination of the lease, the property shall be inspected in accordance with the terms of the lease, and if found in proper condition, security deposit returned to tenant. If there is a dispute between the parties arising from the condition of the premises, and such dispute cannot be resolved, broker may follow the provisions as outlined in 122 of this Title (relating to duration of duty of escrow).

122. Duration of duty of escrow.

(a) *Termination of transaction.* Escrow or trust accounts shall be maintained by the broker until the consummation of the transaction or until a prior termination thereof which does not involve a dispute between the parties to the transaction. In the event of such dispute, the broker shall retain the money in escrow until the dispute has been resolved, except that if that possibility appears remote without legal action, the broker may, after placing the amount in escrow at the disposal of a court, petition the court to interplead the rival claimants.

(b) *Failure to consummate.* If the seller principal fails or is unable to consummate the transaction, his broker, even though he has earned a sales commission, may not place a claim against any portion of the funds advanced which he had placed in escrow, but shall seek payment of such amount directly from his own principal.

123. Termination of business of broker.

The obligations imposed under 121—128 of this Title (relating to escrow requirements) shall continue in the event of death, incompetency, bankruptcy, or other interruption or termination of the business of the broker.

124. Installment land purchase contracts.

In the case of installment land purchase contracts, the transaction shall not be deemed consummated until buyer has been afforded the opportunity, by means of acknowledgment by the seller on or affixed to the sales contract, to record the contract.

125. Sale of cemetery property.

In the case of the sale of cemetery property (lots) the transaction shall be deemed consummated when the buyer received a copy of the sales contract.

126. Multiple listing agreements.

(a) *Delivery to listing broker.* If deposit monies are delivered by a buyer to a listing rather than selling broker, the duty to escrow falls entirely on the listing broker.

(b) *Delivery to selling broker with notice.* If deposit monies are delivered by a buyer to a selling broker with prior notice that such broker intends to pay over such monies to the listing broker, the listing broker, rather than the selling broker, has the duty to escrow such funds. The notice, to be sufficient shall include the following elements:

(1) Explanation by the selling broker to the buyer of his agent status and his disclosure of the identity of the listing broker.

(2) Statement that the listing broker is a real estate broker licensed in this Commonwealth who is required to escrow funds advanced by the buyer.

(3) Signed acknowledgment by the buyer of his receipt of the information in paragraphs (1) and (2) of this subsection.

(4) Acceptance of cash deposits by the selling broker are only on behalf of the listing broker. If the money is tendered by check, the selling broker should request the designation of the listing broker as payee.

(c) *Delivery to selling broker without notice.* If deposit monies are delivered by a buyer to a selling broker without the notice required by subsection (b) of this section that such broker intends to pay over such monies to a listing broker, the selling broker, rather than the listing broker, is under the duty to escrow such funds.

127. Nature and description of escrow account.

(a) Monies required to be escrowed shall be placed by a broker in an escrow or trust fund account which shall be separate and distinct from such business of the broker or personal accounts, or both.

(b) Such account shall be in a bank or recognized depository, indicate on its face that it is a separate escrow or trust fund account, designate the depositing broker as trustee and provide for the withdrawal of funds without previous notice. In case of corporate or partnership broker account, the officer named in the broker's license of such corporation or partnership shall be designated as its agent to make the required deposits and withdrawals and keep the necessary records. The employing broker, including, in the case of a corporation or partnership, the broker named in the license of such corporation or partnership, may authorize, in writing, any employe to deposit funds in the escrow account of the broker. An associate broker or salesman, by express written authority of such employing broker, may be authorized to withdraw funds from the escrow account for payments properly chargeable to the escrow account. In the case of a check for withdrawal of such funds, the signature of the employing broker as drawer of the check shall constitute the necessary written authority.

(c) In connection with a specific transaction, a special escrow account in which the signatures of additional parties are required, may be opened, subject to the other requirements of this section.

(d) If the funds received by a broker which shall be held in escrow are deposited in a banking or other similar depository account which bears interest, such interest shall be held, accounted for, and transferred *pro rata* in the same manner as the principal amount.

(e) Brokers should deposit monies in interest earning accounts if the agreement of sale contemplates a holding period of more than six months.

(f) Every broker shall keep records of all funds deposited in escrow by him which records shall indicate clearly the date and from whom he received money, the date deposited, the dates of withdrawals, and other pertinent information concerning the transaction, and shall show clearly for whose account the money is deposited and to whom the money belongs. All such records and funds shall be subject to inspection by the Commission. Such separate custodial or trust fund account shall designate the real estate broker, as trustee, and such account shall provide for withdrawal of funds without prior notice.

128. Commingling and immediate deposit.

A broker shall deposit escrow funds in a trust account in the manner required by law and this Chapter by the next business day following their receipt. However, if directed to do so in writing by the buyer or offeror, a broker may hold an uncashed check for longer than the above prescribed period pending the acceptance of the offer, although he shall also specifically disclose this fact to the seller or offeree before the acceptance is given.

FEES

131. Applicants and licensees.

The following is a list of fees to be paid by applicants and licensees:

Designation	*Amount (Dollars)*
Application for examination as broker	25.00
Application for re-examination as broker	10.00
Application for examination as salesman	20.00
Application for re-examination as salesman	10.00
Application for examination as limited broker	25.00
Application for re-examination as limited broker	10.00
Application for licensure as limited salesman	5.00
Application for licensure as corporation or copartnership	25.00
Application for licensure as branch office	10.00
Application for licensure as salesman or broker on reciprocal licensure basis	25.00
Reissue of original broker or salesman license	10.00
Reissue of renewal license card as salesman or broker	5.00
Reissue of original branch office license	10.00
Reissue of branch office renewal license card	5.00
Certification of status as licensee	5.00
Biennial registration as broker	25.00
Biennial registration as salesman	20.00
Biennial registration as branch office	20.00
Biennial registration as limited broker	25.00
Biennial registration as limited salesman	5.00

132. Refunds.

No fees will be refunded. However, applicants for admission to an examination who shall in writing withdraw their applications prior to the deadline date of the examination requested will be entitled to a refund of the examination fee.

REAL ESTATE EDUCATION

141. General requirements.

(a) Except as otherwise provided in this section or in 146 of this Title (relating to education equivalent), real estate education sufficient to qualify an individual for a broker's examination shall comprise a minimum of 16 semester credits in the areas of study set forth in this Chapter of schools approved by the Commission as meeting the standards of responsible ownership, administration, curriculum, instruction and physical plan specified in these provisions.

(b) A broker applicant shall receive four credits towards his educational requirement and a salesman applicant shall receive two credits towards his educational requirement for a bachelor degree or a degree the Commission deems to be the equivalent thereof.

142. Areas of study.

The real estate education required by 141 of this Title (relating to general requirements) shall embrace the following areas of study:

(1) The concept of private property in relation to the constitutional powers of Federal and State Governments, such as their powers of eminent domain, taxation, escheat and the State police powers.
(2) Types of property.
(3) Types of real property interests and restrictions.
(4) Methods of transferring real property interests.
(5) Transfer instruments, including the following:
  (i) Lease.
  (ii) The contract of sale and deed of conveyance.
  (iii) Assignment.
(6) Financing real estate transactions, including the following:
  (i) Techniques, installment land sale, sale leaseback, mortgage, etc.
  (ii) Institutions.
  (iii) Instruments.
(7) The mortgaging process, including the following:
  (i) The mortgage market and supporting role of government agencies.
  (ii) Principles of mortgage risk analysis, property valuation, operating costs of properties.
  (iii) Origination, servicing, prepayment and renewal of mortgages.
  (iv) Mortgage foreclosure and rights of respective parties.
  (v) Transfer of mortgages.
(8) Settlement, including mathematics in real estate transactions.
(9) Role of the real estate agent, including the following:
  (i) Principles of agency.
  (ii) Statutory requirements of State licensure and other statutory and regulatory restrictions on the nature of the agency of the broker.
  (iii) Legal rules governing broker compensation.
  (iv) Listing agreements.
  (v) Professional ethics.
(10) Real estate development including the following:
  (i) Incentives to real estate investment and development provided by industrial and commercial development and urban renewal programs and various tax laws on Federal, State and local levels.
  (ii) Zoning and other governmental restrictions on land development.
(11) Real estate appraisal, including valuation concepts and practice.
(12) Real estate management, including all phases of property management.

143. Colleges and universities.

(a) Degree institutions approved by the Department of Education and colleges and universities accredited by such agencies as the Middle States Association of Colleges and Secondary Schools or the American Association of Collegiate Schools of Business shall be deemed to be approved schools and credits granted by such colleges or universities shall be accepted by the Commission to the extent of the number of credits earned in real estate courses.

(b) Institutions approved in this manner shall provide upon request of the Commission a statement containing a description of real estate courses given.

144. Real estate schools.

(a) Schools other than those specified in §35.143 of this Title (relating to colleges and universities) which offer instructions in real estate shall comply with the requirements of this section.

(b) Eligibility to conduct a school for real estate education requires the production of satisfactory evidence to the Commission of the moral and financial responsibility of its sponsors. Applicants for school approval shall satisfy the following requirements:

(1) All sponsors of a proposed school and, in the case of a corporation, and each officer and director who will be directly connected with the conduct and operation of educational program shall be at least 21 years of age with a background of good moral character, including the absence of any conviction for the crimes set forth in Section 11 of the act (63 P.S. §441).

(2) Each sponsor, member, officer or director of an applicant embraced by the terms of this section shall file with the Commission two letters of reference from responsible persons, providing information of his integrity and of any previous experience in the administration or operation of an educational program.

(3) Each application for school approval, and if approved, each annual application for renewal, shall be accompanied by a surety bond to the Commonwealth conditioned for the protection of the contractual rights of real estate students in an amount computed in accordance with the following formula:

Year of Operation	*Factor Number 1*		*Factor Number 2*
First	Number of real estate students anticipated	x	Amount of semester tuition
Subsequent years	Number of real estate students enrolled previous year	x	Amount of semester tuition

(4) The amount of bond required by paragraph (3) of this section shall in no event be less than $10,000. The following Private Real Estate School Contract Bond attached hereto as Exhibit D and made a part of this regulation is exemplary of the standards of this section.

(c) *Certificate of approval.* A certificate of approval shall be granted to the particular school for the specific ownership constituency, each specific school location and the specific name designated in the application for approval. At all times, the certificate shall be displayed on the school premises in a position, where it can be readily viewed by students and visitors alike. Any change in ownership, school location or school name shall be submitted for approval to the Commission at least 90 days in advance of the effective date of the proposed change.

(d) *Fictitious names.* The ownership of schools that propose to use fictitious names in connection with the names or designations of the schools shall register the fictitious names in accordance with the provisions of the act of May 24, 1945, P.L. 967, as amended (54 P.S. §28.1 et seq.) prior to the submission of the application for approval and evidence of such registration shall be submitted to the Commission with the application for approval.

Exhibit D
PRIVATE REAL ESTATE SCHOOL CONTRACT BOND

To accompany Application for an approval as a Private Real Estate School

Know all men by these Presents, that the applicant for said approval__________(name of applicant) with school located at __________(street)__________(municipality) __________(county) as principal and__________(name of Surety Company) with principal office in Pennsylvania located at __________(street)__________(municipality) __________(county) as Surety are held and firmly bound unto the Commonwealth of Pennsylvania for the benefit and protection of the students of said principal, in the sum of Ten Thousand Dollars ($10,000), lawful money of the United States of America, to be paid to the said Commonwealth, its certain attorneys or assigns, to which payment well and truly to be made, we do hereby bind ourselves, jointly and severally, our heirs, executors, administrators, successors, and assigns firmly by these presents.

Signed, sealed with our seals, and delivered this_____day of__________in the year of our Lord, 19____.

WHEREAS, the above bounden principal desires to operate its school at the place set forth above in the manner required both by its express contracts with its students as well as by the provisions of the Real Estate Broker's License Act, the Act of May 1, 1929, P.L. 1216, as amended, and the regulations promulgated thereunder by the State Estate Commission;

NOW THEREFORE, the condition of this obligation is such that if upon and after the issuance of the approval of said school, pursuant to the aforementioned application, the above bounden principal shall fully and faithfully observe the express provisions of all the contracts with its students and the provisions of all the laws of this Commonwealth and the rules and regulations promulgated by the State Real Estate Commission, then this obligation shall be void; otherwise it shall remain in full force, virtue and effect;

And the obligors, jointly and severally, for themselves, their heirs, executors, administrators, successors and assigns do agree with the Commonwealth of Pennsylvania, for the benefit and protection of the students of said principal that upon breach of this bond by reason of violation of any contract with any student or failure of such Principal to observe laws and rules and regulations which may be evidenced inter alia, by the suspension, revocation, or any other determination of the approval aforesaid under the provisions of the Act of May 1, 1929, supra, the Commonwealth of Pennsylvania may maintain action upon this bond for the benefit of such students; provided however, in no event shall the aggregate liability of the surety for all such breaches exceed the sum of this bond.

IN WITNESS WHEREOF, the parties have hereunto set their hands and seals the day and year first above written.

ATTEST:

____

(PRINCIPAL) (SEAL)

__________________________By __________________________

(PRESIDENT) (SEAL)

ATTEST:

____

(SURETY) (SEAL)

__________________________By __________________________

(ATTORNEY-IN-FACT, SURETY) (SEAL)

Address:

____

Approved as to form and manner of execution

By__________________________

Deputy Attorney General

Date: __________________________

145. Administration.

Except as otherwise provided in this Chapter, every school other than those specified in 143 of the Title (relating to colleges and universities) shall meet the following administrative requirements:

(1) *Director.* Each application for school approval shall designate an individual as Director of the School, in responsible charge of its operation, who shall meet the following requirements:
  (i) Be a qualified instructor in real estate.
  (ii) Devote at least 1/2 of the school day to performance of administrative or supervisory duties, or both.
  (iii) File with the commission three letters of reference from previous employers setting forth his previous experience in educational administration and supervision, teaching and any other activity related to education and indicating the location and length of service for each.

(2) *Teaching load.* The maximum teaching load per teacher shall not exceed the ratio of one teacher to 60 students per hour and 300 students daily. A teacher shall not teach more than 20 50 minute classes weekly. Teachers with a teaching load at or near the above maximum amount shall not devote more than 20 hours weekly to additional responsibilities in connection with the operation ana conduct of a school.

(3) *Fees.* All fees shall conform to the following:
  (i) Fees charged by a school shall be specified separately and shall be reasonable and in proportion to the quality and the amount of the services provided in exchange for such amounts. If additional fees are charged for supplies, materials or books needed in course work, they shall be itemized by the school and such articles shall upon payment therefor become the property of the student.
  (ii) The fees and the consideration for them shall be stated in a student contract approved by the Commission. The contract also shall expressly state the policy of the school regarding the return of fees in instances when a student is dismissed or withdraws voluntarily.
  (iii) The following Private Real Estate Enrollment Contract attached hereto as Exhibit E and made a part of this regulation is exemplary of the standards of this paragraph.

(4) *Records.* Records shall be maintained in the following manner:
  (i) Each school shall establish and maintain complete, accurate and detailed financial records which shall include date pertaining to assets, liabilities, sources and amount of income and the character and amount of expenditures. These records shall be kept current and available for their inspection during regular school hours by one or more representatives of the Commission.
  (ii) Each school shall permanently establish and maintain for each individual student a complete, accurate and detailed record, which shall include the total number of hours of instruction undertaken or satisfactorily completed in the areas of study prescribed by this Chapter, classified by curriculum courses, student attendance, and scholastic achievement.

(5) *Attendance.* Requirements and responsibilities with respect to attendance shall be as follows:
  (i) Each school shall keep attendance records for each student for a three year period. Attendance records shall be kept current and available for inspection by Commission representatives during regular school hours or upon request.
  (ii) No student shall receive credit for a course towards the educational requirement, unless he provides the Commission with the certified transcript showing that he has passed the course and attended at least 80% of the classroom time allotted for such course.
  (iii) Falsification of attendance records by the real estate school or refusing to provide a student with attendance records when requested, shall be grounds for the suspension or revocation of the Commission's approval of the school.

Exhibit E
PRIVATE REAL ESTATE ENROLLMENT CONTRACT

In consideration of the ____________________ (Name of School) herein referred to as the "School" accepting me as a student and giving me the instruction specified in its ____________________ Course, (Fall)(Spring) 19____(Day)(Evening) Class, according to the curriculum of the "School", I agree to pay the ____________________ ____________________ (Name of School) or order the sum of __________ dollars as an enrollment fee at the signing and execution of this agreement and the balance of the tuition of __________ payable as follows __________ herewith and __________ (weekly)(monthly) in advance until the total sum of __________ has been paid in full. No portion of the enrollment fee paid at the time of signing and execution of this agreement is subject to cancellation and no refund will be made of any part of said enrollment fee. In addition, I agree to acquire according to the current catalog all books, tools and supplies to pursue the above course, for which __________ is applied herewith.

I further agree to abide by all of the rules and regulations of the "School" as may be established from time to time in connection with said course and if I do not do so, I may be excluded from classes and denied further instruction.

The "School" shall have the right to discontinue instruction and cancel this agreement at any time for violation of rules or unsatisfactory advancement, or if I should refuse to take the instruction offered, in which case the "School" shall refund the unearned portion of the tuition paid, in accordance with the refund schedule of the current catalog.

The "School" has the right to substitute any study or laboratory work in connection with its course when changing conditions in the field of study necessitates such change within the judgment of the "School".

And further the undersigned does (do) hereby authorize and empower the prothonotary or any attorney of any Court of Record of Pennsylvania, or elsewhere, to appear for and to enter judgment against the undersigned for the above earned tuition if not paid when due, with costs of suit, release of errors, without stay of execution, and with five (5) percent added for collection fees; and the undersigned does (do) hereby waive and release all relief from any and all appraisements, stay or exemption laws of any state, now in force, or thereafter to be passed. The undersigned agree(s) to be (jointly and severally) bound by the obligation and warrant(s) to confess judgment herein set forth.

NOTE: ____________________ (Name of School) is not bound by oral agreement or representation other than those specified in this contract and the current catalog.

IN WITNESS WHEREOF, I (We) have hereunto set my (our) hand(s) and seal(s) this ________ day of __________ __________ 19____ .

______________________________	______________________________
(Witness)	(Name)

(If applicant is a minor, parents or guardian must sign)

______________________________ 19__	______________________________
	(Parents or Guardian)

The ____________________ (Name of School) in accordance with the terms mentioned, herewith agrees to enroll the undersigned for the ____________________ Course in its (Fall)(Spring)(Summer) 19____(Day)(Evening) Class.

______________________________	______________________________
(Counselor)	(Educational Director)

(6) *Advertising and prospectus information.* No school shall provide information. No school shall provide information to the public or to prospective students which is misleading when, taken as a whole, there is a distinct probability that it will deceive the class of persons whom it is intended to influence. The following specific cases of advertising, because of their common tendency to mislead, shall receive special attention from the schools:

(i) No school shall use any name other than its approved name for advertising or publicity purposes; nor shall any school advertise or imply that it is recommended, endorsed or accredited by the Commission, the Department of Education or this Commonwealth; but such school may indicate that it has been registered by the Commission to provide instruction in real estate subjects.

(ii) A school shall not apply to itself either as part of its name or in any other manner the designation of college or university in such a way as to give the impression that it is an educational institution conforming to the standards and qualifications prescribed for colleges and universities by the State Council of Education, unless it meets such standards and qualifications.

(iii) Printed catalogs, bulletins, pamphlets, and other forms of prospectus information shall be specific and accurate with respect to prerequisite educational training or experience requirements for admission to the school or courses, the curriculum, the graduation requirements, the tuition, and all other fees or charges. Copies of any form of prospectus information shall, prior to use, be submitted to the Commission.

(iv) No school or agent of the school shall offer special inducements or discounts or make or imply any guarantee of employment, conditional or otherwise, to any student or prospective student.

(v) No school or class shall solicit students to enroll by means of advertisements in the "help wanted" or other employment columns of newspapers or other publications.

(vi) No school or agent of a school shall guarantee that successful completion of the school's courses will result in the student's passing of a real estate licensing examination.

(vii) No school shall advertise or otherwise offer a "money back" guarantee, or engage in other advertising which deceives, misleads, or degrades the dignity of the real estate profession.

(7) *Curriculum.* (The curriculum of schools shall meet the following standards:) Every course shall receive prior approval from the Commission before the Commission will grant credit for such course. Additionally, the curriculum of each school shall meet the following standards:

(i) The curriculum of courses of any real estate school shall be such as to enable a student to cover all the areas of study prescribed in 142 of this Title (relating to areas of study).

(ii) The curriculum shall be capable of completion in a period not to exceed one academic year. An academic year shall mean a period of not less than eight nor more than ten consecutive months.

(iii) In its application for approval or renewal, each school shall specify the group of courses planned to satisfy the requirements, as applicable, with a sufficient description of each course to show its intended coverage of the prescribed areas of study. In conjunction with the application for approval of a course, the school shall submit a copy of the text, manual and other written teaching materials to be used in teaching such course.

(iv) Within 30 days after completing the instruction for a course, the teacher of the course and the director of the school shall certify to the Commission that the course has been taught in substantial compliance with the school's previously submitted description of the course.

(v) No course shall consist of more than five classroom hours per day, unless alternatively, such course consists of five consecutive days of at least 30 hours of instruction.

(8) *Instruction.* Instruction in any school approved by the Commission shall be provided by a teacher who meets the following requirements:

(i) *Moral character.* Each teacher shall be a person of good moral character.

(ii) *Educational qualifications.* Each teacher shall be any of the following:

(A) A real estate broker licensed in this Commonwealth with a minimum of five years active practice in the areas of study which he proposes to teach.

(B) A person holding a degree from an accredited college or university with a minimum of 12 semester credits of course work in the areas of study intended to be taught, and possessing such other qualifications and experience which the Commission deems sufficient to qualify such person to teach in the area for which he seeks approval.

(C) An individual who, in the opinion of the Commission, possesses an educational and experience background substantially equivalent to that required in paragraph (8)(ii)(B) of this section.

(D) An individual who has been duly appointed member of the State Real Estate Commission for a period of not less than two years and not presently serving on the Commission.

(iii) *Teachers.* Teachers shall receive prior approval from the Commission. Approval shall be obtained by each teacher for each course he desires to teach.

(9) *School plant.* Every school, except any correspondence school approved by the Commission for the limited purposes set forth in 145 (10) of this Title (relating to correspondence courses), shall have and maintain a school plant meeting the following standards:

(i) The premises, equipment and facilities of the school shall conform to all applicable safety and sanitary requirements prescribed by the Commonwealth and of the political subdivision in which it is located. The buildings of schools located in Philadelphia, Pittsburgh, and Scranton shall be approved for safety by the Bureau of Fire Inspections of the respective cities. Buildings of schools located elsewhere shall be approved by the Department of Labor and Industry of this Commonwealth as meeting the standards of the Fire and Panic Act (35 P.S. §1221 *et seq.*). A statement of certificate of building approval shall accompany any application for school approval filed with the Commission.

(ii) The artificial lighting facilities shall provide a minimum of 50 foot candles of illumination on the horizontal work surfaces of indoor areas used for instruction purposes.

(iii) There shall be a minimum of 15 square feet of floor space and 150 cubic feet of air space per student in each indoor area to be used for instruction.

(10) *Correspondence courses.* Correspondence courses covering the areas of study prescribed in 142 of the Title (relating to areas of study) may be taken by any person who by reason of hardship cannot attend a school for classroom instruction, but any school offering such course shall, to the extent applicable, meet all other standards prescribed by this Chapter and require that at least 50% of the passing grade of its corresponding students be based on scores obtained on proctored examinations.

(11) *Charges.* To enable the Commission to administer and enforce the provisions of this Chapter, schools other than colleges and universities shall be required to pay the following charges which are refundable:

(i) $50 for Initial approval of the Real Estate Commission to conduct a school for real estate education.

(ii) $50 for approval by the Commission for each additional school location.

(iii) $25 annually for renewal of certificate.

146. Education equivalent.

(a) The Commission shall deem the following three classes of persons as eligible for consideration as having received the equivalent of the educational requirements specified in this Chapter:

(1) Any person who has satisfactorily completed the number of semester credits, specified in §141 of this Title (relating to general requirements) and defined in 1 of this Title (relating to definitions) of course work in real estate subjects in any college or university or any real estate school operated under the auspices of a real estate board prior to September 22, 1966.

(2) Any person who has received a professional education, whether before or after September 22, 1966, which involves instruction in subjects substantially similar to those required by this Chapter.

(3) A real estate broker who is not licensed as such in this Commonwealth and who is applying for a broker's license in this Commonwealth shall be given two semester credits for each year of active practice as a real estate broker during the five year period immediately preceding the date of his application.

(b) Any person who has satisfactorily completed less than the number of semester credits specified in 141 of this Title (relating to general requirements) and defined in 1 of this Title (relating to definitions) of course work in real estate subjects in any college or university or any real estate school operated under the auspices of a real estate board prior to September 22, 1966 shall complete only the required number of semester credits of course work specified in 141 of this Title (relating to general requirements) in an approved school.

147. Evidence of compliance with education requirement.

Any person applying for the Real Estate Brokers' License Examination shall submit certification from the institution in which courses in real estate have been satisfactorily completed.

148. Limited licensure educational requirements relating to cemetery sales.

The professional education requirement for individuals qualifying for limited brokers' license in the cemetery field shall be as follows:

(1) Any professional education obtained by an applicant applying for a limited broker's license at an administrative or sales school conducted under the auspices of the National Cemetery Association or similar association will be considered by the Commission as qualifying towards the professional education requirements, if, however, the applicant supplies the Commission with a certification or transcript from the educational institution which establishes that the applicant has obtained a passing grade in qualifying courses of study.

(2) The educational requirements after the effective date of January 15, 1967 for limited brokers shall be four credit hours in a regularly approved real estate school or accredited college or university or one management and one sales course conducted under the auspices of the National Cemetery Association or similar association.

OUT OF STATE LAND SALE OPERATIONS

151. General requirements.

(a) Any broker, developer or subdivider herein after referred to as "applicant", who proposes to engage in sales of a promotional nature in this Commonwealth of property located outside of this Commonwealth shall submit to the Commission, for its approval before doing so, full particulars regarding such property and proposed terms of sale, and they and their salesmen shall comply with such rules and regulations, restrictions and conditions pertaining thereto as the Commission may impose. Expenses reasonably incurred by the Commission in investigating and inspecting such property and proposed sale thereof in this Commonwealth shall be borne by the applicant. No broker or developer or salesman shall in any manner refer to the Commission or to any official or employe thereof in selling, offering for sale, or advertising, or otherwise promoting the sale, mortgage or lease of any such property, nor make any representation whatsoever that such property has been inspected or approved or otherwise passed upon by the Commission, or by any State official, department or employe.

(b) Applicants approved to engage in sales set forth in this Chapter shall notify the Commission at least ten days in advance of the date, time and place of all efforts to sell or advertise through parties or reception or other group media.

152. Nonresident requirements.

(a) Every nonresident applicant shall also file an irrevocable consent that suits and actions may be commenced against such applicant in the proper court of any county of this Commonwealth in which a cause of action may arise, or in which plaintiff may reside, by the service of any process or pleadings authorized by the laws of this Commonwealth on the State Commission in Harrisburg, Pennsylvania, such consent stipulating and agreeing that such service of such process or pleadings on the Commission shall be taken and held in all courts to be as valid and binding as if due service had been made upon the applicant personally within this Commonwealth.

(b) In case any process or pleadings are served upon the Commission, it shall be by duplicate copy, one of which shall be filed in the office of the Commission and the other immediately forwarded by certified mail to the main office of the applicant against which the process or pleadings are directed.

153. Offering statements.

(a) The Commission also requires the applicant to prepare and deliver at its own expense, to each prospective purchaser in the Commonwealth an offering statement which shall be revised annually. The offering statement shall be approved by the Commission and shall contain a detailed description, price and terms of the offer as well as financial information disclosing assets and liabilities of the applicant. The offering statement shall also inform prospective purchasers of any tax liabilities, basis for guarantees, public transportation facilities, terrain details, climate, proposed and existing improvements, roads, water supply, public utilities, any objectionable condition of air, sight or terrain, sewage disposal facilities, recreational and community facilities and the distances to any nearby populated area.

(b) The offering shall also set forth on the front page in large bold face type or italics, the following statement:

The State Real Estate Commission's requirements of this broker, developer or subdivider does not constitute approval of the land being offered for sale or lease. The State Real Estate Commission has not in any way passed upon the merits of such offer.

154. Review and approval of documents.

The following information and its documents shall be furnished annually to the Commission in report form for its review and approval:

(1) Name of owner, including the following:
- (i) Names and addresses of all owners of partners.
- (ii) Lists of all officers and holders of 10% or more of total subscribed or issued stock of the corporation.
- (iii) Copy of most recent certified audit of records including financial statements.

(2) Names of subsidiary organizations or companies.

(3) Name of development.

(4) Address of development.

(5) Addresses of administrative offices.

(6) Representatives of this Commonwealth including a list of all sales offices and personnel in this Commonwealth.

(7) Status of property, including the following:
- (i) Owner of the land.
- (ii) Whether land is free and clean.
- (iii) If land is mortgage whether the mortgage is assignable including the following:
  - (A) Whether individual lots can be released.
  - (B) Cost per lot.
- (iv) Whether there are any judgments against or unpaid taxes due on the land.
- (v) Whether abstracts or title policies will be furnished.

(vi) Copy of type of deed used.
(vii) Whether deeds are issued in fee simple.
(viii) Whether there is additional charge for issuing a deed.

(8) Improvements completed, including the following:
(i) Paved streets.
(ii) Sidewalks.
(iii) Street lights.
(iv) Public utilities.
(v) Whether improvements are paid for.
(vi) Tax rates.
(vii) If no improvements, plans for completion.
(viii) If FHA approved, copy of approval.

(9) Whether bond has been posted with any governmental authority to guarantee completion of promised improvements, including the following:
(i) Specification for what purpose.
(ii) Amount.
(iii) Name of bonding company.
(iv) How this bond will protect the purchasers from the Commonwealth.
(v) Certified copy of the bonds used.

(10) Sewage, including the following:
(i) Sanitary sewers.
(ii) Storm sewers.
(iii) Whether water mains or individual wells are necessary.
(iv) Whether septic tanks are necessary.
(v) If septic tanks are necessary, whether they are authorized by appropriate government authorities.
(vi) Whether level of land and type of soil is suitable for septic tanks.

(11) Drainage, including the following:
(i) Whether land is dry.
(ii) Copy of the drainage plan of the engineer.
(iii) Depth of water table.
(iv) Depth of average well.

(12) Zoning restrictions, including the following:
(i) Copy of topographical map.
(ii) Copy of State Board of Health Percolation Test one hole per five acres where septic tanks are used.

(13) Advertising, including the following:
(i) Size of lots offered.
(ii) Price and terms of sale.
(iii) Whether these lots are large enough for building purposes that would comply with zoning requirements.
(iv) If and where plot is recorded.

(14) Location, including the following:
(i) Aerial photo showing exact area with at least one mile of bordering properties.
(ii) How far property is presently from the following:
(A) Highway.
(B) Incorporated town.
(C) Major shopping area.
(D) Industrial area including type and size.
(E) Transportation including bus and train.
(F) Schools, public, trade, parochial, or private.
(G) Lighted streets.

(H) Type of pavement and curbs.
(I) Fire protection.
(J) Garbage and trash removal.
(K) Police protection.
(L) Airport and airlines operated therefrom.

(15) Current selling price of lots in adjoining area and owners of these lots.
(16) Financial arrangements, including the following:
(i) Whether down payment will be placed in escrow and terms of release of down payment.
(ii) Type of financing obtainable and percent of interest charged.
(iii) Closing costs, specifying for what.
(iv) Specific listing of carrying charges.
(v) Types of contracts used.

155. Affidavit of consent to service of jurisdiction.

The following affidavit of consent to service of jurisdiction attached hereto as Exhibit F and made a part of this regulation is exemplary of the requirements of 154 of this Title (relating to review and approval of documents).

POST SUSPENSION AND REVOCATION

161. Posting of Commission Action.

(a) The broker who is a sole proprietor or the broker of record for a partnership or corporation must post notice of Commission action suspending the license of the employing broker. The notice will be provided by the Commission and must be posted at the main office and all branch offices of the suspended broker. The notice must be prominently posted and externally visible at all times during the period of suspension.

(b) Failure to post this notice as required shall constitute grounds for further suspension or revocation of the responsible party's license.

Exhibit F
AFFIDAVIT OF CONSENT TO SERVICE OF JURISDICTION

That the undersigned ____________________ (give legal designation of applicant, individual, partnership, corporation) does hereby irrevocably consent that any action brought against the above named applicant in the proper court of any county of the State of Pennsylvania or in which the plaintiff in such action may reside and that in the event proper service of process cannot be had upon such applicant in any such proceeding in such county, service of any process may be made therein by the sheriff of such county by the service of any process or pleadings authorized by the Laws of Pennsylvania on the Real Estate Commission, hereby stipulating and agreeing that such service of such process or pleadings on said Chairman shall be taken and held in all courts to be valid and binding as if due process has been made upon said applicant in the State of Pennsylvania.

President ____________________________________

Secretary____________________________________

Corporate Seal

Witness _____________

Personally appeared ____________________before me the undersigned notary public in and for the above named county and state, the day and date above named, and acknowledged that execution of the foregoing instrument to be the voluntary act and deed of such applicant for the purpose therein set forth (if applicant is an individual, strike out the following) and that they are the President and Secretary, respectively, of such corporation and are duly authorized to execute the foregoing instrument.

(Seal)

State of__________SS
COUNTY OF___________

CERTIFICATION

We, the undersigned, do hereby certify that the statements made, exhibits furnished, financial statements and answers to questions are true and correct and that we realize that any untrue or incorrect information supplied to this Commission or infraction of the Rules and Regulations, or restrictions and conditions which the Commission may impose in granting approval to the applicant shall be cause for immediate suspension or revocation of any and all privileges granted said applicant to operate in the State of Pennsylvania.

Authorized Signature______________________(Seal)

Sworn to and subscribed
____

before me this______day of______19____
____

Notary Public

Code of Ethics
National Association of Realtors®

The NATIONAL ASSOCIATION OF REALTORS® adopted its Code of Ethics in 1913. Through the years it has proved helpful and beneficial to everyone in the real estate business because it contains practical applications of business ethics and statements of good practices that everyone in the business should know and carefully follow. A real estate business is only as good as its reputation, and reputations are built on sound business practices and fair dealings with clients, other real estate brokers, and the general public.

Preamble

Under all is the land. Upon its wise utilization and widely allocated ownership depend the survival and growth of free institutions and of our civilization. The REALTOR® should recognize that the interests of the nation and its citizens require the highest and best use of the land and the widest distribution of land ownership. They require the creation of adequate housing, the building of functioning cities, the development of productive industries and farms, and the preservation of a healthful environment.

Such interests impose obligations beyond those of ordinary commerce. They impose grave social responsibility and a patriotic duty to which the REALTOR® should dedicate himself, and for which he should be diligent in preparing himself. The REALTOR®, therefore, is zealous to maintain and improve the standards of his calling and shares with his fellow-REALTORS® a common responsibility for its integrity and honor. The term REALTOR® has come to connote competency, fairness, and high integrity resulting from adherence to a lofty ideal of moral conduct in business relations. No inducement of profit and no instruction from clients ever can justify departure from this ideal.

In the interpretation of his obligation, a REALTOR® can take no safer guide than that which has been handed down through the centuries, embodied in the Golden Rule, "Whatsoever ye would that men should do to you, do ye even so to them."

Accepting this standard as his own, every REALTOR® pledges himself to observe its spirit in all of his activities and to conduct his business in accordance with the tenets set forth below.

As approved by the Delegate Body of the Association at its 67th annual convention, November 14, 1974.

The Code of Ethics was adopted in 1913. Amended at the Annual Convention in 1924, 1928, 1950, 1951, 1952, 1955, 1956, 1961, 1962, and 1974.

Where the word REALTOR® is used in this Code and Preamble, it shall be deemed to include REALTOR-ASSOCIATE®. Pronouns shall be considered to include REALTORS® and REALTOR-ASSOCIATE®s of both genders.

Article 1

The REALTOR® should keep himself informed on matters affecting real estate in his community, the state, and nation so that he may be able to contribute responsibly to public thinking on such matters.

Article 2

In justice to those who place their interests in his care, the REALTOR® should endeavor always to be informed regarding laws, proposed legislation, governmental regulations, public policies, and current market conditions in order to be in a position to advise his clients properly.

Article 3

It is the duty of the REALTOR® to protect the public against fraud, misrepresentation, and unethical practices in real estate transactions. He should endeavor to eliminate in his community any practices which could be damaging to the public or bring discredit to the real estate profession. The REALTOR® should assist the governmental agency charged with regulating the practices of brokers and salesmen in his state.

Article 4

The REALTOR® should seek no unfair advantage over other REALTORS® and should conduct his business so as to avoid controversies with other REALTORS®.

Article 5

In the best interests of society, of his associates, and his own business, the REALTOR® should willingly share with other REALTORS® the lessons of his experience and study for the benefit of the public, and should be loyal to the Board of REALTORS® of his community and active in its work.

Article 6

To prevent dissension and misunderstanding and to assure better service to the owner, the REALTOR® should urge the exclusive listing of property unless contrary to the best interest of the owner.

Article 7

In accepting employment as an agent, the REALTOR® pledges himself to protect and promote the interests of the client. This obligation of absolute fidelity to the client's interests is primary, but it does not relieve the REALTOR® of the obligation to treat fairly all parties to the transaction.

Article 8

The REALTOR® shall not accept compensation from more than one party, even if permitted by law, without the full knowledge of all parties to the transaction.

Article 9

The REALTOR® shall avoid exaggeration, misrepresentation, or concealment of pertinent facts. He has an affirmative obligation to discover adverse factors that a reasonably competent and diligent investigation would disclose.

Article 10

The REALTOR® shall not deny equal professional services to any person for reasons of race, creed, sex, or country of national origin. The REALTOR® shall not be a party to any plan or agreement to discriminate against a person or persons on the basis of race, creed, sex, or country of national origin.

Article 11

A REALTOR® is expected to provide a level of competent service in keeping with the Standards of Practice in those fields in which the REALTOR® customarily engages.

The REALTOR® shall not undertake to provide specialized professional services concerning a type of property or service that is outside his field of competence unless he engages the assistance of one who is competent on such types of property or service, or unless the facts are fully disclosed to the client. Any person engaged to provide such assistance shall be so identified to the client and his contribution to the assignment should be set forth.

The REALTOR® shall refer to the Standards of Practice of the National Association as to the degree of competence that a client has a right to expect the REALTOR® to possess, taking into consideration the complexity of the problem, the availability of expert assistance, and the opportunities for experience available to the REALTOR®.

Article 12

The REALTOR® shall not undertake to provide professional services concerning a property or its value where he has a present or contemplated interest unless such interest is specifically disclosed to all affected parties.

Article 13

The REALTOR® shall not acquire an interest in or buy for himself, any member of his immediate family, his firm or any member thereof, or any entity in which he has a substantial ownership interest, property listed with him, without making the true position known to the listing owner. In selling property owned by himself, or in which he has any interest, the REALTOR® shall reveal the facts of his ownership or interest to the purchaser.

Article 14

In the event of a controversy between REALTORS® associated with different firms, arising out of their relationship as REALTORS®, the REALTORS® shall submit the dispute to arbitration in accordance with the regulations of their board or boards rather than litigate the matter.

Article 15

If a REALTOR® is charged with unethical practice or is asked to present evidence in any disciplinary proceeding or investigation, he shall place all pertinent facts before the proper tribunal of the member board or affiliated institute, society, or council of which he is a member.

Article 16

When acting as agent, the REALTOR® shall not accept any commission, rebate, or profit on expenditures made for his principal-owner, without the principal's knowledge and consent.

Article 17

The REALTOR® shall not engage in activities that constitute the unauthorized practice of law and shall recommend that legal counsel be obtained when the interest of any party to the transaction requires it.

Article 18

The REALTOR® shall keep in a special account in an appropriate financial institution, separated from his own funds, monies coming into his possession in trust for other persons, such as escrows, trust funds, clients' monies, and other like items.

Article 19

The REALTOR® shall be careful at all times to present a true picture in his advertising and representations to the public. He shall neither advertise without disclosing his name nor permit any person associated with him to use individual names or telephone numbers, unless such person's connection with the REALTOR® is obvious in the advertisement.

Article 20

The REALTOR®, for the protection of all parties, shall see that financial obligations and commitments regarding real estate transactions are in writing, expressing the exact agreement of the parties. A copy of each agreement shall be furnished to each party upon his signing such agreement.

Article 21

The REALTOR® shall not engage in any practice or take any action inconsistent with the agency of another REALTOR®.

Article 22

In the sale of property which is exclusively listed with a REALTOR®, the REALTOR® shall utilize the services of other brokers upon mutually agreed upon terms when it is in the best interests of the client.

Negotiations concerning property which is listed exclusively shall be carried on with the listing broker, not with the owner, except with the consent of the listing broker.

Article 23

The REALTOR® shall not publicly disparage the business practice of a competitor nor volunteer an opinion of a competitor's transaction. If his opinion is sought and if the REALTOR® deems it appropriate to respond, such opinion shall be rendered with strict professional integrity and courtesy.

Article 24

The REALTOR® shall not directly or indirectly solicit the services or affiliation of an employee or independent contractor in the organization of another REALTOR® without prior notice to said REALTOR®.

Index

References are to Licensing Law Sections